MAKING CAMP

The Complete Guide
for Hikers, Mountain Bikers,
Paddlers & Skiers

MAKING CAMP

CAMP

The Complete Guide
for Hikers, Mountain Bikers,
Paddlers & Skiers

by Steve Howe, Alan Kesselheim,
Dennis Coello, and John Harlin

BACKPACKER
THE MAGAZINE OF WILDERNESS TRAVEL

Published by
The Mountaineers
1001 SW Klickitat Way, Suite 201
Seattle, WA 98134

THE MAGAZINE OF WILDERNESS TRAVEL

© 1997 by *BACKPACKER* magazine
33 East Minor Street
Emmaus, PA 18098

10 9 8 7
5 4 3 2 1

Published simultaneously in Great Britain by Cordee, 3a DeMontfort Street, Leicester, England, LE1 7HD

Manufactured in the United States of America

Edited by Kris Fulsaas
Cover design by Helen Cherullo
Book design by Alice Merrill
Book layout by Jacqulyn Weber
Typography by Jennifer Shontz
Cover photograph: Ouzel Lake, Mount Redoubt, Washington
    (Photo: ©Cliff Leight)
Illustrations by Dawn Peterson

Library of Congress Cataloging-in-Publication Data
Backpacker's making camp: the complete guide for hikers, mountain bikers,
    paddlers & skiers / by Steve Howe . . . [et al.]
        p.   cm.
    ISBN 0-89886-522-0
    1. Camping. 2. Backpacking. 3. Boats and boating. 4. All
terrain cycling. 5. Skiis and skiing. 6. Snowshoes and
snowshoeing. I. Howe, Steve, 1954- . II. Backpacker.
GV191.7.B33 1997   97-25346
796.51—dc21   CIP

☘ Printed on recycled paper

Contents

Searching for Camping Nirvana

AUGUST 1993. SOMEWHERE IN CANOE HEAVEN. It was my first solo wilderness trip. I had been paddling and portaging all day, and the sun was starting its descent. My intended campsite was just around a long hotdog-shaped island up ahead. On the map it looked ideal: The dot that marked the site dangled like a red polished nail on the end of a finger, a flat peninsula on the south side of a small island.

I parked my canoe and got out to explore the established campsite. This was one of those rare cases where reality proved much better than even the most beautiful preconceived notion. From the water, a large ramp of rock sloped up to a sunny plateau, fringed with a string of tall pines. Like a custom-built home, the campsite had all the elements of the perfect living space: a flat square tent spot with a waterfront view, a central cooking area with a neat fire ring, and a large rock slab for swimming in the lake. It even had a bush full of ripe blueberries and a pair of perfect food-hanging trees.

By the next morning, I was so enamored with my backwoods home that I decided to stay there rather than move to a different lake each night as I had originally planned. Call me lazy, but this campsite was too good to leave. The next 3 days were warm and sunny as I lounged about my private island. I read and wrote, napped and skinny-dipped, and a few times each day I paddled around the nearby marshes looking for moose. Flawless weather, the consummate campsite, and no pressing agenda. Camping nirvana.

More often than not, camping is portrayed as what happens at the end of days spent hiking, paddling, biking, ski touring, or snowshoeing. But it's really much more than that. Camping is the time when you make

A mountain-bike trailer on a single-track trail in Montana.
(Photo: ©Dennis Coello)

your home in the backcountry. It's a temporary home, to be sure, but you have—or should have—the basics that you need to live "out there." You hope that the place itself provides you with everything else (inspiration, opportunities for photography, personal space, whatever you are searching for). Sure, camping is sleeping on the ground, peeing in the woods, eating from food-encrusted bowls, and getting rained on. It's living with hat hair, washing dishes with sand, and using duct tape a dozen different ways to fix your gear. But it's also the time that you can strip to the basics and leave all the extra mental and physical "stuff" at home. What people invariably say is, "I have *everything I need* in my pack" . . . or in the canoe or on a bike or on a sled. It's amazing to be able to live with so little.

In all my wilderness rambles, I have yet to replicate those wonderful 3 days in the Boundary Waters, where I did nothing other than "camp." In fact, if you ask any of the authors of this book, they'll say that wilderness camping is rarely such a smooth and effortless affair. There are all sorts of pesky things that can get between you and camping paradise: rain, snow, cold, heat, bugs, bears, blisters, a leaky tent, grumpy companions, bad food . . . the list goes on and on. The simple fact is that the camping gods are not always in your court. But that only means you have to be so well prepared that you can laugh at the rain and avoid the blisters, leaks, and bad food. Common sense, a positive attitude, and good planning will see you through most backcountry challenges.

That's where this book comes in: It's all about the art of camping. There are hundreds of sport-specific books out there that will teach you the particulars of outdoor activities: how to pack your backpack, paddle with a J-stroke, fix a flat tire, or carve a telemark turn. This book focuses on making your home in the backcountry. You may be an ace skier, for instance, but without some winter camping skills, you'll never get far from the lift lines.

This book is the collaborative effort of four outdoor specialists who have mastered the art of camping in their particular genre. Each writer, through years of trial and error, has amassed a wealth of tips for making outdoor life enjoyable and safe.

Chapter 1, written by **Steve Howe** with assistance from Dennis Coello, John Harlin, and Alan Kesselheim, is directed to backpackers. However, it contains information useful to all backcountry adventurers regardless of mode of travel, so read it in addition to the chapter specific to your outdoor activity of choice. There are well-honed tips about pretrip planning, choosing a campsite, setting up camp, and enjoying your sojourn.

Steve is the Southwest editor for *BACKPACKER* magazine. "Backpacking's really the only way to get into core wilderness areas. With a pair of boots, a pack, and some dreams, you can almost always pick an intriguing spot on the horizon, say to yourself 'I want to see that,' and then go there," he says. Steve's assignments have led him to wild places all over the continent, from the Alaskan tundra to the Sonoran Desert. "My camping expertise comes largely from the fact that I've made almost every mistake at least once."

Chapter 2, written by **Alan Kesselheim**, deals with the particulars of travel by canoe, kayak, and raft. Because watercraft allows you to carry more than other backcountry modes of transportation, you can often tuck in more (and heavier) items that can make camping downright luxurious.

Alan is a freelance writer and contributing editor of *BACKPACKER*. He and his wife twice paddled across Canada on fourteen-month trips that included wintering over in the Far North. He has also been on raft and canoe trips on many of the major river systems in the United States, and has kayaked extensively on the Great Lakes. Alan has written several books about his adventures, including *Water and Sky* and *Going Inside*. Alan continues to enjoy water travel with his wife and three young children.

Chapter 3, by **Dennis Coello**, offers suggestions to those who would embrace the outdoors on a mountain bike. Dennis explains how to get all the gear you need onto your bike (yes, it can be done) and offers his insights about backcountry camping with a mountain bike as your companion.

Dennis is one of the country's best-known mountain-bike specialists and the author of twelve cycling books. Dennis has literally pedaled all around the world on both pavement and single track, but backcountry bike touring is his passion. "The thing I love about bike travel is that you can jump from wilderness to town life in the space of a few hours, so you're free to travel lighter and schedule resupplies in valley towns."

Chapter 4, by **John Harlin**, covers the unique challenges of snow camping. John gives advice on choosing a site, setting up your tent so it will withstand wind and snow, obtaining water, drying gear, and many other concerns of critical importance to those who would make their home outdoors in the world of frost and snow.

John is *BACKPACKER*'s Northwest editor. Skiing has been John's joie de vivre since he was three years old. He later branched out into winter mountaineering and backcountry skiing, and he snow camps with a passion. In Colorado's Rocky Mountain National Park, where John was a professional climbing and ski guide, he taught weeklong winter mountaineering courses. He has also snow camped in the Andes, the Alps, the Brooks Range, the Alaska Range, the Coast Range, the Cascades, the Sierra, the Canadian and American Rockies, the Adirondacks, the Poconos, and the Mexican volcanoes. John says that quite frankly he prefers sleeping on a tropical beach with his wife to pitching camp with his mates after dark in a blizzard at high altitude. But you have to take what the mountains give you, and snow is an important part of the package. Might as well love it all!

In the end, Alan Kesselheim says it best: "Camping is about learning to be comfortable as a nomad." When the comforts of home are confined to what you can take with you—whether by pack, boat, bike, or sled—you're free to roam any far-flung place on the map. And when you finally find that perfect, idyllic campsite of your dreams, like I did in northern Minnesota that summer, call it home and stay for a while.

—Kristin Hostetter
Equipment editor
BACKPACKER magazine

CHAPTER I

BACKPACKING

—

At Home on the Trail

Steve Howe with sections by John Harlin,
Alan Kesselheim, and Dennis Coello

NO MATTER HOW YOU are planning on enjoying the backcountry—by foot, by water, by bike, by ski, or by snowshoe—there are some basic steps to making sure that your home away from home will give you what you need each night. The suggestions in this chapter apply to all activities. Considerations specific to backpackers are indicated by headings, so if you are using some other mode of backcountry travel, you can skip those particulars. While considerations for paddlers, mountain bikers, and snow campers are found in following chapters, most readers will want to read this first chapter, because it covers the basics.

Every backpacker has a special wilderness moment they cherish. The one I recall most vividly was many years ago, during a brief rest break atop Electric Pass, a high crest in the Maroon Bells–Snowmass Wilderness of Colorado. My brother, a friend, and I stood dumbstruck by a huge diorama of beauty and adventure; to hike down from this vista, we faced several hours of very hard effort. We were tired. It was late. Camp was a long way off. We were just realizing how big the Elk Range really was, and just how ambitious our plans were. We were fourteen years old. It was our first unsupervised trip, not an adult in sight to check our enthusiasm . . . or correct our mistakes.

Desolation Wilderness, Sierra Nevada, California (Photo: Jeff Scher © ERG)

Back across the intervening twenty-eight years, I can still recall the bodily thrill of vast wilderness, waiting adventure, and the looming unknown. Ranks of 14,000-foot peaks surrounded us. Everywhere lay hints of special places to be discovered, soaring cliffs, deep glades, and the echo of roaring water. The possibilities seemed endless.

Backpacking was the only way we could have reached this destination. There was no road nearby, thankfully, although there were plenty everywhere else. The trail we'd taken was too rough for a mountain bike or horse. There were no navigable rivers nearby, and not enough snow to make skis or snowshoes feasible. The only currency that allowed anyone access to Electric Pass was honest physical effort, and we had spent that coin freely, carrying too much, making wrong turns, hiking too fast, resting too long, making a daylong procession of naive mistakes.

We were tired kids, but we were lucky, because our parents weren't worriers. They didn't object whenever we loaded up a week's worth of camping and climbing gear to disappear into what most people would consider a "hostile" wilderness. The 1970s backpacking boom hadn't dawned yet. There were very few guidebooks and no magazines on the sport. Guides and outfitters were few and far between. Outdoor education and wilderness therapy programs were almost unknown. And so every peak and valley in the Elk Range was ours for the grabbing, but we had to figure it all out ourselves. We rarely reached our planned destination on the first trip.

Looking back, I consider that lack of information and guidance a blessing. It forced us to be self-reliant, to think for ourselves. We picked the places that looked coolest based on what we saw from roads, ski areas, maps, and the occasional airline flight. We made mistakes, lots of them, and the effort they cost us imprinted the lessons far more deeply than reading or instruction could. We quickly learned how to stay oriented, read compasses, gauge the difficulty of a trail from map contours, and look behind us frequently to keep from getting confused on our return trip.

It may seem ironic that I'm recalling all this with nostalgia, considering that this is a manual about how to avoid mistakes. But it's not, really. What follows is simply a compendium of suggestions, checklists, and priorities gleaned from the scattered mayhem of a thousand small backcountry mishaps, the benefit of woeful experience translated into a series of general hints, nothing more. You are still free to choose your own challenges, adopt your own style, find your own wilderness paradise, make your own mistakes.

In the decades since I looked down off Electric Pass, I've been fortunate enough to visit magnificent wildernesses from Alaska to Peru, but I can't say those exotic journeys were any more rewarding than my early, fumbling trips through Colorado's Elk Range. I still make plenty of mistakes, but I've learned how to avoid some of the big ones, and developed kits and systems for solving others more quickly. I've learned to enjoy the physical challenge of pushing hard on the trail, but I've also learned that backpacking isn't about winning, or chalking up miles and summits as if they were trophies. It's about enjoyment, exercise, and, most of all, nature and your place within it.

Surprisingly, I've learned that wilderness camping is easy. Look at it this way: Neanderthals pulled it off routinely with way worse gear than we've got. Humans were made for wilderness living. We've just forgotten it briefly. It consists of the same motions we go through every day in the city, but tailored to slightly different ends. Despite all the outdoor marketing, backpacking isn't about gear, glamour, or risk; it's about simplicity, and backpack camping does not take an expert, it just takes common sense.

So learn from this book, but don't hesitate to try things your own way. Choose your own routes. Head down a trail you know nothing about. Don't be afraid to make mistakes; just try to keep them manageable, and be ready to solve them on your own. Once you do that a few times, you'll gain a wonderful sense of outdoor confidence, one that frees you to do adventures you might otherwise have never considered.

There's still plenty of wilderness out there. Wilderness lovers tend toward the grumbling attitude that hordes are always on our heels, but there's no shortage of magnificent solitude. Backcountry "crowds" are, happily, only an isolated and readily avoidable phenomenon. To find wilderness solitude, you need only pick those anonymous map spaces between the roads, rivers, and trails, or turn 180 degrees from the crowded overlook, and ask yourself, "What might be out there?"

Then go.

PRETRIP PLANNING

Itinerary

Any journey begins at home, and no one ends up at a fine wilderness campsite without some planning. No matter where or how you travel and camp in the backcountry, always carry six things: food, shelter, clothing, travel equipment, emergency gear, and a plan.

Because there are so many magnificent places you might end up, it's a good idea to begin any trip by asking yourself the basic questions of why, where, what, who, and when:

Why are you going? Are you looking for solitude, companionship, exercise, contemplation, wildlife, scenery, photos, easy backwoods living, or a challenging mountain? Because these goals involve trade-offs, it's worth clarifying your priorities. Don't try to do too much in a single trip; an overly full itinerary guarantees disappointment.

Perhaps the most common source of backcountry group strife arises over conflicting trip goals and differences in personal style. If you have one subgroup that prefers a precise and regimented approach to camping, and another that eschews watches altogether and lets mood dictate the routine, you're in for a long trip.

Before you start, it's critical to communicate about trip goals, personal ambitions, and camping styles. Once underway, keep those lines of communication open. Little conflicts have a way of festering if they aren't discussed. Most important, be flexible and willing to compromise.

Where can you find the experience you're seeking? By looking into guidebooks, magazines, and maps and inquiring with friends and federal and state land managers, you can usually come up with a significant list of destinations. The problem is usually one of choosing, rather than finding, a place to go. Keep in mind you don't need the largest or most distant wildland to have an enjoyable backcountry time. The wilderness experience is as much a matter of imagination and curiosity as geography.

What type of trip do you want? For instance, you might embark on a 5-day loop, a weekend out and back along the same trail, a rugged cross-country exploration, or a base camp–oriented trip with daily forays. It's worth choosing a trip that's not so grueling that you can't enjoy the scenery, so that you can arrive in camp reasonably sound and not spend all your time recuperating.

Who to go with? First, find friends or companions whose company you enjoy, and who can schedule the same time off as you. But along with the rewards of friendship, be aware that differing abilities and expectations can lead to friction, especially when the going's tough. The stresses of wilderness living and travel are a real test of a group's ability to compromise, negotiate, and tolerate personal quirks. There is certainly no trusty formula by which groups succeed, but there are several things to consider before departure that will go a long way toward ensuring that success.

As you contact your potential companions, make sure you communicate thoroughly. Whether it's an afternoon hike or a monthlong expedition, by the time you reach the trailhead everyone should have roughly the same goal and schedule. Also, if you're assembling companions for some dream trip you've been planning for ages, keep in mind they may not share your zeal. If you're cooking up an epic journey, remember to choose an appropriate group for that trip, or another trip for the group. Misfitting the two is a recipe for trouble.

Because solo backpacking can commit you to completing a difficult journey, it's not recommended for novices or those whose backwoods confidence is low enough to keep them constantly nervous. But for those who prepare well and travel carefully, solo trips offer a profound experience, since the lack of companions tunes you into the surrounding environment even more. Make sure to leave your travel schedule and expected return time with a trusted friend who can contact authorities, should you be disabled or injured in the backcountry.

When to visit? Most of us have restricted vacation schedules, so the best time to go backpacking is usually whenever you can. Most of the time, that means whenever we've got time off from work. It's also worth keeping track of incoming weather systems before leaving for your trip, so you don't get pounded by a "surprise" storm that's been forecast for the last week. But you could also phrase this question as "When *not* to visit." Once you've narrowed down a few destinations, check with the relevant land management agency to see if you may be arriving during an inopportune time. For example, misanthropes won't find solitude in Great Smoky Mountains National Park during the peak of autumn colors, or in

When choosing traveling companions, make sure that everyone under-
stands the goals, the schedule, and the anticipated rigors (or laid-back
aspects) of the trip. (Photo: ©Marypat Zitzer)

Canyonlands at Easter. Likewise, you won't find easy camping in the
Rockies in December, or in Death Valley in August. Your timing will also
affect important details like water availability. During desert summer,
you may have to carry your entire water supply. At 8 pounds per gallon,
and one to two gallons per person per day, the availability of water can
make or break your plans.

Food

After a long day of exercise and fresh air, one's appetite is sharpened to a
razor edge, and eating becomes a true joy of camping—which is fortunate because, in the backcountry, food is fuel, and replenishing your de-
pleted calories is a necessary chore. Athletic performance and personal
enjoyment are improved if your menu is not only nutritious, but light in
weight, and simple to prepare.

Despite undercooked noodles or burned entrees, camp food rarely tastes anything less than wonderful. But choosing your food for proper nutrition, estimating the correct quantities, and organizing menus for longer trips can test the patience and self-confidence of the most experienced adventurer. Healthy, nutritious meals and a varied menu are the underpinning for everything from strong morale to safe decisions. Conversely, bland, inadequate, and unvaried menus can lead to insufficient energy, and trips fraught with bickering. Ironically, food is often the aspect of trip preparation that gets slighted.

Weightwise, food is a logistical challenge, and a key one at that: You *must* have enough food, but food also weighs a lot, and you can easily overestimate your caloric needs. Be forewarned: No matter how hard you try, the food supply always seems to be "off." Too much, too little, wrong stuff. You starve on the day you hike uphill in the cold, and belch your way along on sunny afternoon descents. The group that ate like hogs last autumn won't touch anything but juice next summer.

You'll never get the food exactly right, but you can get it close. As a general starting point, figure that a 5-foot-9-inch-tall male who weighs 180 pounds will probably eat 2½ pounds of dehydrated food per day. A 5-foot-5-inch-tall female who weighs 120 pounds will probably eat 2 pounds per day. Increase these per-day weight estimates slightly if you're relying on meats, cheeses, or anything canned, because these items weigh much more than dehydrated foods. Decrease these per-day weight estimates slightly if you are using a lot of freeze-dried food. It'll help future menu preparation efforts if you keep informal records of your supplies on various trips.

▲ ▲ ▲

Things NOT to Do with Camp Food
- Try to save money while shopping.
- Supply yourself from the corner quick mart.
- Take less so you'll lose weight through forced dieting.
- Improve your companion's eating habits by bringing only health foods.
- Forget it at the trailhead.
- Lose it to critters or water damage.

Using a home food dehydrator is inexpensive, allows you to plan a menu that is both varied and nutritious, and provides trip food economically. (Photo: ©Marypat Zitzer)

Too frequently, trip menus are made up of instant hot cereal packets, foil-pouch meals that all taste the same, and serving portions that befit an in-flight meal. There is no need to succumb to this tyranny of bland and unhealthy provisions.

It is possible to eat much as you would at home, if you're willing to spend time dehydrating your food supplies, find alternatives to the amount of meat in your diet, and devote a little extra camp time to cooking. A food dehydrator is an investment that will return culinary dividends for years of backcountry travel and cut down dramatically on trip expenses. Fruits, vegetables, snacks, sauces, even entire entrees can be dried and packed into the larder to liven up trail days.

Even without a dehydrator, you can create nutritious expedition meals from common (and relatively inexpensive) supplies purchased at the grocery store. Think about the meals you enjoy at home and adapt them slightly to fit the restrictions of your wilderness travel—length of itinerary, need for resupplies, shortened cooking times, availability of water, and so on.

Why not make home-style spaghetti, chili, stew, or burritos? Dehydrate spaghetti sauce, refried beans, salsa, and other ingredients at home, then add hot water in the field to create home-style meals. A few fresh spices give camp meals added zest. Prepackaged rice and noodle dinners are grocery-store items that can be used as a base to build tasty meals. Soup and sauce packets are lightweight additions that expand the menu.

If you do use prepackaged food, you can still add flavor and nutrition by complementing meals with some selected fresh vegetables (onions, garlic, carrots, and cabbage all keep well and boost a meal considerably). Take along a complete spice kit. A solid selection includes salt, garlic powder, pepper, dill, cumin, curry, oregano, basil, and cinnamon. Compact condiments (mustard, soy sauce, Tabasco) add taste without taking much space. Store them in leakproof plastic bottles with screw-on lids.

The surest path to the food doldrums is to inflict on yourself a monotonous diet. Develop a meal rotation that varies basic staples—pasta, rice, beans, grains. Mix up the trail snack varieties. Buy several kinds of cheese. (Hard cheese like Parmesan and sharp cheddar tend to keep longer than soft varieties.) Include both hot and cold cereals. Have a dessert now and then. Add some treats for times when morale needs an indulgence.

Before heading for the outdoors, leave as much potential garbage behind as possible, repackaging anything that comes in glass or cardboard containers. (Using resealable plastic bags or tying a knot instead of using a twist tie helps eliminate those ubiquitous little wires found in littered campsites across the continent.) Plan your menu to avoid leftovers, or later reuse them, to minimize garbage in the backcountry.

Backpacking Tips: Cooking Gear

You can approach the weighty matter of camp cuisine from various angles. Most backpackers choose a moderately spartan philosophy for their camp menus. Or you can go ultralight by skipping the stove and eating fruit, granola, and food bars, an approach that works very well in hot climates, where the last thing you want after a long hike is a nice, hot meal. Or, if these styles seem to be needless self-denial, you can organize a gourmet kitchen and consider food as a significant part of your backpacking experience. For most hunger-maddened backpackers, simple one-pot breakfasts and dinners, well prepared and spiced, are more than adequate, as long as portions are big enough.

At its simplest, your camp kitchen might be only a couple of butane/propane canisters with a screw-on burner, a covered cook pot, and a spoon. You can actually get full-on boiling and simmering action from such a tiny kitchen package, at a total weight of roughly 2 pounds. A windscreen, blackened pots, and heat channelers further increase the efficiency of any given stove setup, and the three in combination will halve your cooking time. Gourmands will be pleased to note that two-burner backpacking stoves are on the horizon and, should you choose, you can lay on all the backcountry ovens, double boilers, and espresso makers you want. But at first, you're probably better off going simple.

Shelter

Shelter is second only to food in the hierarchy of backcountry necessities. And when most people think of wilderness shelter, tents come to mind. It's important to pick a tent suitable to the climate you'll be traveling in, and the party you'll be hiking with. For example, a four-person group in the rainy Northwest might need a large dome tent and several tarps for group cooking shelters and gear storage, while a solo backpacker in the Sonoran Desert could get by with a compact mosquito-net shelter, or a small tarp. The longer and more remote your trip, the more you should err on the side of shelter overkill, since prolonged storms could descend, and hiking out to the trailhead is less of an option.

It's best if your sleeping bag is rated slightly warmer than necessary for the conditions you plan to travel in, to allow you the option of venting, rather than making you cinch and curl to stay sufficiently warm just for the sake of saving a few ounces in your pack. A secure, protected, dry feel is important to overnight recovery, helping you sleep deeper and stave off sickness in chillier climates. A margin of error in your sleeping bag's rating also allows you more freedom of movement, because you can strip down to light, comfortable, and quickly dried overnight clothes.

Clothing

Temperature, weather, and your body's own heat output vary wildly during a 24-hour trail day, so outdoor clothing faces a significant challenge covering all the bases. Any system needs to be versatile enough to ventilate you during midday trail exertions, dry quickly after high-sweat periods, keep you warm during the sedentary chill of morning and evening, and keep precipitation at bay when the weather's screaming. Because adventurers can't haul a closet-sized wardrobe, the only way to obtain the necessary versatility is by carrying clothes that can be combined in varying layers: few for warm periods, or all for those times when you need serious protection. Most modern outdoor clothing is designed and manufactured to be used in this kind of layering system.

Next to your skin, base-layer long underwear is made to transport moisture away from the body, using body heat to "push" water vapor outward, and dry quickly after exercise. Thicker insulating layers lie over these thin base garments. Sweaters and vests, usually several worn in varying combinations, provide dead air space between you and the surrounding environment. Atop all this, "shell" layers cut wind, repel water, and shed snow, protecting both you and your underlying insulation. Generally speaking, the two most important layers are the base and shell, because they have to handle the intense demands of sweating skin and harsh climates.

Outdoor clothing is usually made of synthetic fabrics that absorb little or no water, such as polypropylene, polyester, or specially treated nylons. These "hydrophobic"—or water-hating—fabrics, found under a confusing variety of brand names, are justifiably popular as base layers, because they dry quickly and "wick" moisture away from the skin. In wet conditions, synthetic fabrics are the choice. Cotton, a very popular fiber for casual clothing, gets extremely cold when wet, and dries slowly. In colder, wetter climes, the evaporative cooling of cotton clothing is a recipe for hypothermia, the dangerous lowering of the body's core temperature. Consequently, cotton should be avoided for backcountry use, except in hot deserts like the American Southwest, where cotton is workable. Accept wool grudgingly; it's warm, but weighs a lot and dries slowly. Wool may be the most common fabric for good socks, but to maximize comfort, backpackers need clothes that dry rapidly with only body heat, and only the high-tech synthetic fabrics seem to accomplish that, particularly in humid conditions.

In colder climates, take more clothes than you think you'll need, simply because most of us aren't used to standing around in the outdoors 24 hours a day. On the trail day after day, between remote camps, you get no chance to step into a warm room—such as what you'd find at a ski hill or after a day hike—so you need more clothing in order to maintain your comfort level when relaxing in those kinds of meteorological settings. The ideal is to take enough clothes so you can stay warm even if you can't start a campfire or your tent leaks. Whether you're doing an afternoon hike or a monthlong odyssey, always have enough clothes to allow you to experience a wet, tired, hungry epic and at least have a reasonably comfortable time.

Once you've used the layering system a bit, and understand how to regulate your layering comfort for a given condition, you'll become quite secure even in adventurous, committable weather. Modern technical outdoor clothing works very well. Just add a weatherproof tent, and you can stay warm and dry in most conditions. The main thing is to take enough clothes in cooler weather. An extra jacket or a pair of mittens can provide a lot of additional comfort for very little added weight.

Base layers. If there's one clothing layer you shouldn't scrimp on, it's the one next to your skin. A sweating backpacker can put out two quarts of water per hour in hot temperatures. Your base-layer clothing must be able to transport that cooling sweat away from your body, and dry quickly enough that you won't be shivering during the chill evening hours around camp. Consequently, most base-layer "long underwear"–style clothing for active outdoorspeople is made of specially treated polyesters. These fibers don't absorb water, and the fabric weaves are designed to "wick" moisture away from the skin. Although base-layer clothing typically costs much less than insulating or shell layers, it's suitable for everything from summer jogging to winter camping. Long-sleeved, zip turtlenecks and "sport tights" (rather than classic "long underwear" bottoms) offer the most adaptability for varying temperatures and uses.

Insulating layers. The intermediate insulating layers between base and shell are marginally less critical to your comfort, but they are still important, particularly for harsher climates or seasons. Wooly-looking knit fleeces made of polyester (Polartec is the most commonly found brand name) are the most popular insulators for backpacking, because they are durable, provide effective dead air space, layer easily, and dry quickly. Wool sweaters also insulate well, but they weigh more, dry slowly, and tend to wear under constant abrasion. For lounging around camp in colder climates and seasons, a parka or vest filled with down or synthetic fill is a luxury well worth its weight, but for summer travels such a garment is usually excessive. In wet weather, down must be kept dry.

Shell layers. Outer shell clothes are typically made of tightly woven nylon. For all-around use, the waterproof-breathable coatings and laminated fabrics such as Gore-Tex, Entrant, H2No—and numerous other confusing brand names—work best, because they handle moderate rain well, yet still breathe sufficiently to avoid giving you a sweat bath during trail exertions. Waterproof-breathable shells actually steam sweat and wetness out through the porous fabric, so you can dry out underlayers by wearing them around camp after a storm or high-sweat periods. The major drawbacks to waterproof-breathable shell wear are high price and the fact that it does not repel prolonged, heavy rain as well as coated, fully waterproof fabrics.

All shell jackets, regardless of fabric or season, should be easily ventable, to adjust for sweat output, and have attached hoods to help insulate the head against its considerable potential for heat loss. You should also be able to don or doff your shell pants without removing the boots you typically wear, and they should not restrict knee lift during hill climbs.

Clothing the extremities. To round out your clothing, all the additional pieces you may need are a sun hat, a cold-weather hat, gloves or mitts, and good-quality socks. Wool remains popular for hats, gloves, and particularly socks, but the polyester fleeces actually perform better for all these uses. Fleece socks stretch less than wool, however, and need to be fit more carefully. On the upside, polyester fleece socks dry overnight, even when soaked, a feat wool socks are hard-pressed to duplicate.

Backpacking Tips: Footwear

Backpacking is all about load carrying and trail miles, two factors that can definitely be hard on feet. Consequently, boots can make or break your trip. Light packs and short, easy trails can be navigated with running shoes, but packs above 20 pounds, and hikes on rougher terrain, call for more protective, supportive footwear. The heavier your average pack weight and the rougher the terrain you'll be traveling, the stiffer and more supportive your boots need to be.

The choosing, fitting, and care of boots are subjects that could fill a whole book in themselves, and so we'll confine ourselves here to a few general hints. First, a proper fit is far and away the most important consideration when choosing boots. Each company's boots, and specific models, are contructed around a wooden foot called a "last." If the manufacturer's last isn't shaped like your foot, then the best-made boots in the world will only be an expensive, durable torture device.

Spend a lot of time choosing and sizing any boots. Resist the temptation to buy hastily. Once you've visited several stores and sampled perhaps a half dozen different pairs, then you can think about which ones were most comfortable. Take along the same sock combinations you plan to wear, because differing socks will greatly affect the fit. You should have enough room in the boot to allow for toe wriggling and swollen feet at the end of the day, but not so much that your feet slop around when you're walking downhill or balancing on unstable slopes. If you're having a lot of trouble finding comfortable boots, consider purchasing separate arch supports or footbeds, since they often provide better contouring where it's most needed.

Once purchased, your boots need to be maintained in order to prolong their life and keep the supple, supportive fit. Protect exposed stitching with commercial seam-sealers, and keep leather boots waterproofed with a wax- or silicone-based treatment. Waterproofing treatments keep your feet drier and prevent leather boots from shrinking or getting uncomfortably stiff and "boardy."

The material of choice for socks, wool has survived far longer against the advance of synthetic polyesters than for other applications because of its resiliency to compression and its overall comfort. But wool socks don't easily dry overnight, a serious drawback because socks are always damp from foot sweat and frequent sock washings are advisable to avoid blisters. The best answer to this quandary is the newer socks made of synthetic fleece. These piece-sewn socks must be fit more carefully than stretchy wool, but they're plenty cushy and guard well against foot friction. Best of all, they get tinder-dry overnight when tossed in the foot of a sleeping bag. Hung from a tent ceiling (deprived of the body's heat pump), synthetic fleece socks retain some moisture, but dry quickly upon being donned and feel warm to the touch in seconds.

Camp shoes not only help save your feet and allow your carpal bones to realign themselves after a day in stiff leather hiking boots, but lightweight, soft-soled camp shoes also save wear and tear on your campsite, because they dig up less topsoil. Camp shoes should be quick-drying, so they'll be comfortable again soon after dewy mornings or if you use them for river crossings and bog wallowing. In warm climates, sports sandals work well, although running shoes seem better suited to most environments. In winter, soft mukluks are the ticket. These fabric-outer pull-on boots are knee-high and, when layered over thick socks or pile booties, they're the most luxurious footwear imaginable, because they're so soft. The knee-high cut lets you posthole around a deeply snowed camp on various errands, yet you can easily remove the mukluk cover for tent entries.

Maps and GPS

You won't enjoy camp if you're wandering around lost, so always carry a current map of the area you're in, along with a compass, and have the ability to use them both. If you need some instruction, take a course from a local outdoors organization or read up on the subject. Once you've had some experience, orienteering is pretty easy, and with little hassle you can practice map and compass skills while traveling. Keep your compass and map quads in a quickly reached location, and refer to them frequently during your travels.

When in unfamiliar areas, make sure you start from the correct trailhead or put-in, and that you remain solidly oriented from there, tracking progress carefully as you go. Particularly in remote regions with poorly "developed" trailheads, it's very common for people to get lost at the very beginning of their trip, but not realize it until their route assumptions no longer fit.

Global Positioning Systems (GPS) are becoming more popular for backcountry navigation, as their weight and price decrease. In featureless or obscured ecosystems like tundra barrens and dense forest, these satellite-oriented devices can tell you exactly where you are standing, and even how far you are from a preselected goal, but they can't tell you which direction you're facing—only a compass can do that. A GPS is positional, a compass is directional. Actually, many GPS units give direction of current travel, but a hiker's pace typically falls below the speed threshold for this function—consequently, GPS units should be considered an adjunct to map and compass skills, not a replacement for them. GPS units also have fairly high battery requirements, so always carry spares. When using a GPS alongside a compass, separate the two by 1 foot or more. You'll note that the compass needle veers when it's brought near the antenna of the GPS. Be careful of inaccurate compass readings.

The Ten Essentials

There are a lot of important items that haven't been covered in the preceding sections, such as sunglasses, flashlight, knife, and first-aid kit. If you forget something on a trip, it'll probably be some critical widget from the Ten Essentials list. Usually it's some single item you have a mental block about, and you tend to forget it over and over. The checklist in the sidebar titled Equipment Checklist for Backpacking should help you avoid any frustrating lapses of memory.

1. Extra clothing. Despite the desirability of packing light, bring one full change of clothes and keep it dry for emergencies.
2. Extra food. Always bring more food than you think you'll need, at least one full day's worth.
3. Sunglasses. These are critical to avoid eyestrain, headaches, and eye injury in high-glare conditions.
4. Knife. A simple pocket knife is a versatile, vital tool.
5. Firestarter. In extremely wet or cold conditions, you may need to start a fire to avoid hypothermia.
6. Matches in a waterproof container. To use a backpacking stove in very wet conditions, make sure your matches stay dry. An alternative is a butane cigarette lighter, which dries easily, lights repeatedly, and is easily warmed in subzero temperatures.
7. First-aid kit. Pack a complete assortment for the type of trip you will be taking; include sunscreen for most types of outdoor activities.
8. Flashlight. Pack a set of spare batteries, too.
9. Map. An up-to-date topographical map is vital.
10. Compass. Know how to use it.

Miscellaneous Gear

Favored luxuries include all those fetishes you don't really need, but consider worth their extra weight—camp slippers, binoculars, lanterns, lounge chairs, umbrellas, star charts, that book you're dying to finish. Keep in mind, however, that time-honored bylaw of backpacking: "If it weighs much, think about leaving it."

▲ ▲ ▲

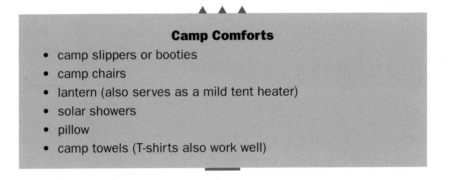

Camp Comforts
- camp slippers or booties
- camp chairs
- lantern (also serves as a mild tent heater)
- solar showers
- pillow
- camp towels (T-shirts also work well)

Backpacking Tips: Packing and Organizing

Once you've got a working plan, it's time to assemble food, shelter, clothing, travel equipment, and emergency gear suitable for your trip. The key defining factor about backpack camping is that it all has to fit on your back, and that, in turn, means there's a lot you can't take. Consequently, every piece of equipment you do consider has to be evaluated on the basis of its weight, size, usefulness, and durability.

Light weight is always important, because every ounce you carry adds up to hundreds of foot-pounds of effort when it's hauled along miles of trail. Small size and compactness are also critical, because everything has to fit in or on your backpack, a volume somewhere between 4,000 and 7,000 cubic inches, or roughly twelve to eighteen gallons. Whatever you carry should also be useful, and preferably versatile enough for several jobs, in order to justify its added payload. Specialty items that may only be used once or twice during a long trip might better be left at home. Durability is important because items you rely on must last through often rough usage. In addition, durable gear is more economical in the long run, because it translates to more trail days per dollar spent, and less eventual trash. But durability also means more weight, and perhaps gentle usage might allow you to travel lighter.

It's worth mentioning here that many backpackers trash their gear through carelessness, rather than sheer mileage. Outdoor equipment has a finite life, and must be maintained. You can keep time-consuming maintenance to a minimum by treating your equipment with respect on the trail. Use it, but don't intentionally abuse it. Zip zippers carefully. Set your pack down easily rather than throwing it. Avoid shoving tent poles into a full stuff sack, lest you rip the nylon canopy. Don't cram items like stoves and headlamps forcefully into your load when packing. Treat your stuff well and most of it will return the favor.

One interesting exercise is to pack only the necessities, everything you "must" take, and weigh that load on your home scale. Then pack everything you're "planning" on taking, and compare the two weights. But remember, you can't afford to scrimp on food, shelter, or clothing.

▲ ▲ ▲

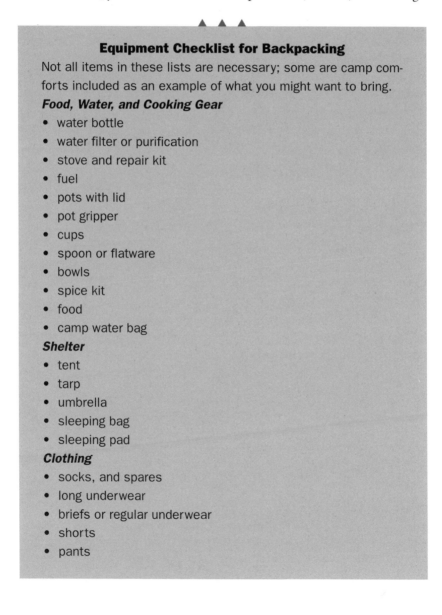

Equipment Checklist for Backpacking

Not all items in these lists are necessary; some are camp comforts included as an example of what you might want to bring.

Food, Water, and Cooking Gear
- water bottle
- water filter or purification
- stove and repair kit
- fuel
- pots with lid
- pot gripper
- cups
- spoon or flatware
- bowls
- spice kit
- food
- camp water bag

Shelter
- tent
- tarp
- umbrella
- sleeping bag
- sleeping pad

Clothing
- socks, and spares
- long underwear
- briefs or regular underwear
- shorts
- pants

- shell pants
- T-shirt
- base shirt
- sweater
- vest
- shell jacket
- sun hat
- warm hat
- gloves or mitts
- camp shoes

Travel Equipment

- backpack
- boots
- trekking poles or hiking staff
- GPS
- a plan

The Ten Essentials

- extra clothing
- extra food
- sunglasses
- knife
- firestarter
- matches in waterproof container (or cigarette lighter)
- first-aid kit
- flashlight
- map
- compass

Miscellaneous (many items optional)

- toiletry kit
- sunscreen
- repair items (spare buckles, sewing needle and thread, nylon cord, wire, duct tape, tent pole sleeve, spare parts, etc.)
- lantern
- camp chair
- star chart
- binoculars
- camera

- book
- tent games
- towel
- solar shower
- nylon cord (tent guy lines, repairs, boot laces)

CHOOSING A CAMPSITE

Where you camp is second only in importance to where you choose to go camping. Your site lies at the heart of your wilderness experience, and how you go about choosing it reflects how you go about everything in the great camping game. Generally speaking, your camp should be a convenient, secure, benevolent place to spend time, and a good view certainly doesn't hurt.

The following tips are all common-sense things. Think about the big picture, and the details will fall into place. Sweat the small stuff too much, and you might forget why you're camping in the first place.

Picking the night's resting spot more than likely occurred while you were looking at the map before beginning the trip or, at the latest, this morning in your last camp. In some parks and wilderness areas, backcountry campsites must be reserved in advance, and in those areas your site selection will be greatly simplified, if not necessarily optimized. In the vast majority of other areas, you're free to choose your own temporary home, but that can be a double-edged sword: you're also free to make your own mistakes. It's a good idea to begin looking for a suitable camp well before dusk, to allow yourself flexibility of choice. Once darkness has fallen, you can waste a lot of time and effort trying to locate and organize a secure, comfortable camp that you can't see clearly. You'll also avoid a lot of environmental impacts if you're not blundering around in the dark, tromping over invisible but delicate vegetation as you look for a flat tent site.

Once you get to the place marked by the X on the map, the first thing to decide is whether you really want to camp there. Is this truly an exciting spot where you can soak up everything you love about the outdoors? Or is it just some arbitrary spot marked on the map that leaves you a little disappointed? If the latter, consider moving on—even back a little—unless you're too bushed or permits/designated campsites require you to sleep there.

But don't just camp in your ideal spot, because the most important variable comes next: What effect will your campsite have on those who follow? If the obvious well-used site is under a tree and the picture-perfect site is in a wildflower meadow, sleep under the tree. If you're near a trail and your favorite site will put your tent smack in the middle of everyone's mountain view, well, don't be rude. If your movements in camp will tear a fragile moss bed, cross that site off the list.

Think long-term. Once you've passed through, you want this place to look just the same as it did when you showed up. And remember that generations of campers will be making the same decisions after you've traveled on. If there are well-used sites, use them so you don't start a trend toward clusters of tent platforms. If it doesn't look as though anyone has been here before, try to stay on bare rock if possible, grassy meadows that can take a little trampling, or forest duff that isn't home to delicate vegetation. Mostly this is common sense, but you must train yourself so that minimizing impact becomes pure habit.

▲ ▲ ▲

Leave-No-Trace Considerations for Choosing a Campsite

- In high-use areas, camp in heavily used sites.
- In pristine areas, camp on durable surfaces that will show no traces of your visit.
- Always avoid sites just beginning to show signs of use, because they can self-recover.
- Always camp, and site your latrine, at least 200 feet from a water source.
- Choose a resistant surface your shoe soles won't tear up or pack down.
- Conceal your camp from others, to minimize visual clutter.
- Your camp should conform to land management plans and zones.
- Camp away from key waterholes, wildlife feeding areas, nests, and dens. Allow the residents access to needed food, water, and shelter.
- Store food responsibly to avoid habituating animals.

With minimum impact in mind, start sorting through the other variables.

View. If you'll be watching the sunset through your tent door, line it up to anticipate that angle. Just being slightly off-angle might keep you from seeing those last minutes—or seconds—of changing light.

Morning sun. Especially if the morning will be chilly (common in the mountains) or if you need an early boost, you might skip the sunset view and instead orient the tent toward the east (usually northeast in the summer) to catch the rising sun. On the other hand, if you intend to sleep in, make sure the sun won't come streaming through the door before your time.

Wind. If the summer breeze is light and you want it for cooling or to keep the bugs at bay, orient the door to windward. If the door is to leeward, you might find a thousand-mosquito reception party each time

For some campers, the view is the most important element in a tent site. Here, an awkward slope was well worth enduring so that the tent door could face a glorious view of the Arrigetch Peaks in the Brooks Range, Alaska. (Photo: ©John Harlin)

When the wind comes up and you're in an exposed area, consider moving to a more sheltered site. (Photo: ©Marypat Zitzer)

you unzip your tent. But if the wind is strong or might become so, orient the small end of the tent toward the wind, the better to deflect its blow. You certainly don't want wind blowing rain straight into your door, nor do you want it buffeting your tent's flapping flanks. It might not be windy when you set up camp, but sometimes the environment will give you strong clues on what to expect. Especially obvious are "flag trees," which have branches growing on one side only. The other side typically faces strong wind, and you'd be wise to consider its prevalent direction before pitching camp.

Drainage. Should rain spout on you overnight, you won't want rising waters to carry you downstream. Nor will you appreciate a mysterious midnight creek flowing into your precious shelter. Avoid water collection zones (divots, gullies, and the like). Try to choose spots where water soaks into the ground rather than collecting on top—pick sandy or loamy soils or absorbent forest duff.

Nearby water. The ideal site has an accessible water source, but you shouldn't camp too close to it. Minimum-impact guidelines suggest camping at least 200 feet from the water so that your impact, from dishes to toilet, is less likely to affect water quality. Also, because lakes and streams are focal points for most wilderness tourists (humans) and natives (wildlife), camping close to the water will likely make you more visible, thus lessening everyone's experience.

If you've planned your trip with water sources in mind, finding water in the wilds should not be too difficult. Rivers and creeks are noted on small-scale maps, but do not count upon seasonal tributaries if rain has been sparse. If you're traveling in dry regions, where water resupply can be nonexistent, talk with others who have gone before and sharpen your lookout for indicators of water: in shady areas up side canyons; near vegetation; at the lowest ground level around. Follow animal tracks in these directions, and human tracks near campsites used before. If you think that your campsite may be more than a few minutes' walk from a water source, plan to gather your evening's water supply at the nearest water source before you continue on to your anticipated campsite.

Bedroom vs. great room. In an ideal campsite, you can stash your gear, cook, and sleep all within a few feet. Trouble is, this concentrates the wear on one place, which may not be a good thing for the environment. Also, if there are hungry critters around, they will be attracted to your cooking area, which also happens to be your sleeping area. So it's typically best to choose one site for your kitchen and dining pleasures, another for sleeping. As usual, let common sense be your guide.

Inclined sleeping. If you're forced to use a sloping tent site, be sure to orient the tent so your head is uphill. Slip a pack or boots at the foot of your sleeping bag to block you so that you don't slide into the tent wall (only a real problem if it's wet). If you're on a sidehill, a pair of boots between you and your partner can do wonders to keep the oaf from rolling on top of you.

Don't molest the site. Do your best to smooth out surface unconformities—protruding rocks, sticks, et cetera—but don't scrape the site level. Get down on hands and knees and pick out the offending items. Old-fashioned trenching, bough breaking, and other site manipulations are totally unacceptable.

After-dark activity. Remember that if you wander away from the tent at night, you'll likely have your flashlight aimed at your feet. Pointy branches at eye level can be a serious hazard. So can crevices or cliffs that can't be seen in the dark. It's hard to imagine how much a campsite transforms once the sun goes down, but change it does.

Bugs, bugs, bugs. If you set up camp early near a marshy area, the bugs may still be hiding. Alas, dinner hours may coincide—yours and the mosquitoes'. Think about bugs to come, not just the bugs of the moment.

Temperature switches. By day, valley floors are typically warmer than hillsides, but at night that warm air floats away and cold air sinks to take its place. That's why you see frost pockets in dips and swales. Do you want to wake up in a frost pocket? You might be better off choosing a sidehill or ridge-top site that's cooler in the evening but warmer come the morning. Equally important is overhead cover. Meadows typically cool off more at night than forest floors because tree branches trap some heat that otherwise radiates straight to the stars.

Anchors. If your tent isn't freestanding, tie out its guy lines and floor. Usually this is done with stakes. But the lowest-impact camping sites—bare rock and loose sand—typically don't hold stakes well. Owners of freestanding tents should take heed of this as well, as many a camper has watched their dome tent blow off a cliff or into a lake. On rock, the only solution is more rock: You'll need enough boulders to do the work your stakes would have. (Don't yank these boulders out of the ground, leaving obvious holes in their wake.) In sand, drive a stake, then place a rock or two on top of it. This is usually much easier than tying straight to rocks. Remember that if the tent gets rained on, it might slacken as the fabric's weave opens; you'll need to tighten the guy lines later, perhaps at night. Keep this in mind when you tie your knots or place your rocks.

Neighbors. If nearby campers have habits different from your own—music making, snoring, fitful sleeping, early rising—you or they might end up hating the camping experience that otherwise could have been pure joy. Try not to crowd your neighbors, always be considerate of them, talk with them about their habits before you start throwing rocks, and try to calm down and tune them out if all else fails. Or go over and join the party if it's keeping you up anyway; you might make new friends. If you anticipate a crowded campground, take a tip from experienced hut users: Bring a set of those cheap foam earplugs available in any hardware store.

Stream noise. The stream may sound like music while you're pitching camp, but the white noise while you're trying to sleep may drive you batty until you're used to it. Consider your nighttime needs before pitching a tent where you can't sleep.

Falling objects. Remember that you'll be spending a number of hours in exactly the same spot; make sure that spot is safe. Falling rocks and dead trees have killed campers around the world. So have seracs, avalanches, tree branches, coconuts, and even giant pinecones. Check overhead to make sure gravity doesn't bring you any midnight surprises.

▲ ▲ ▲

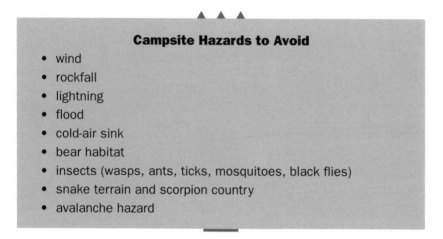

Campsite Hazards to Avoid

- wind
- rockfall
- lightning
- flood
- cold-air sink
- bear habitat
- insects (wasps, ants, ticks, mosquitoes, black flies)
- snake terrain and scorpion country
- avalanche hazard

SETTING UP CAMP

Arrival in Camp

Camp arrival is an important transition during your day, due to the contrast between hot, sweaty travel and the chill onset of sedentary evening. There are as many different ways of sliding into camp as there are ecosystems and outdoorspeople. In hot desert conditions, camp arrival could be as simple as collapsing in the shade, guzzling a half gallon of electrolyte replacement drinks, and not moving until sunset. In winter mountaineering, it could mean you fire up the stove immediately upon arrival to melt snow for hot soup while you layer on clothes and set up the tent. If it's just an average downpour, maybe hang your tarp first and cook for a while beneath it before dealing with other camp organization.

▲ ▲ ▲

Checklist for Camp Arrival

The order of and need for these activities might be different depending on the weather, the site, and your own preferences.

- choose site
- don dry clothes
- gather water
- start stove to heat/purify water
- drink water
- care for feet
- set up tent
- fluff sleeping bag
- store gear
- eat light snack within 45 minutes of arrival
- set up camp kitchen
- cook and eat dinner

Dressing for Camp Comfort

Comfortable camping is largely a matter of taking care of yourself, and the immediate post-exercise period—when you've stopped and are cooling down—is a critical point in your daily self-maintenance. When you are backpacking, you are working hardest during the hottest part of the day and cooling off rapidly in evening, when air temperatures are likewise plunging. You need to dry your clothing very quickly, particularly across the lower back, where you get very sweaty due to the insulation of the pack's back panel. Despite all the high-tech fabrics, dispersing this moisture at the end of a day can be a challenge, particularly in humid environments. Many people chill easily after hard exercise, yet you may be wet for several hours after arriving at a camp.

Upon arriving at camp when it's cool, pile on the middle, insulating layers, because these layers are warm enough to help you avoid chill, yet are breathable enough to move moisture out through the small air pockets in the fabric matrix. Individual water vapor molecules "breathe" out through it all. Consequently, dressing in these thick but breathable layers offers the most comfort for relaxing in camp. If you have sweaty base layers that need to be dried out, black is the most efficient color for your base layers in cooler climates, because it dries so much faster in the sun.

In hot weather, have a dry set of clothes to climb into after a sweaty day. A spare T-shirt and shorts can make life positively civil, and you can hang the soaking-wet stuff on a sun-drenched bush or cactus till it's dry.

In rainy conditions, carry a complete extra set of dry camp clothes that you keep stored in a plastic bag or lightweight dry bag, and pull them out only after your tarps and tent are set up (or you can even save them strictly for sleeping). No matter how wet you get from sweat, humidity, or rain during the day, you can still take refuge in a dry, snug haven of clothing and shelter at the end of the day. Two duplicate base layers are also a pretty ideal combination for longer backcountry trips. You can wear one set while the other's getting washed and dried. That warm, dry core, along with a good hot meal and eventually a secure night's rest, goes a long way toward restoring you after a day's hard exertions.

Rehydrate

After getting into dry clothes, your next priority at a backcountry camp-site, after a day of intense exertion, is rehydrating. If you don't have enough water left in your water bottles, gather water and either purify it (see The Camp Kitchen, below) for cold drinking water or set up the stove and heat water for hot soup or hot drinks—something light and restorative. If you're going to take aspirin or ibuprofen, now is a good time in order to minimize post-exercise stiffness. A large-volume hanging water bag allows you to gather enough water in one trip to satisfy most camp needs right through breaking camp and setting off the next morning.

Backpacking Tips: Caring for Your Feet

After staying warm and dry, and rehydrating, a backpacker's most critical bodily priority is foot maintenance. Feet swell, particularly when pounded for miles underneath weighty packs. They're actually squished out in length and width during every step you take, and this becomes more pronounced under a heavy pack. Hopefully you've maintained your feet during the day, so blisters haven't become painful. But even with the best-fitting boots, your feet will compress and swell and stiffen, and it's reasonable to assume they will arrive in camp in need of recuperation.

Once you've gotten into dry clothes and gotten some liquids into you, it's time to pull off the encrusted boots and malodorous socks, maybe wash your feet, and do some repair. Hopefully you'll have nice, comfy camp shoes to slide into. Then dry—or wash and dry—those well-used socks for the next day's hiking. Given the drying efficiency of modern, synthetic outdoor clothing, getting your clothes dry is rarely a problem—except for socks, those soaked and sweaty, but very critical, protectors of the all-important foot. Take care of this task as soon as possible, to allow maximum drying time for your socks.

Pitching Your Tent

Setting up the tent is a priority, especially if weather conditions are bad. Of course, you've practiced at home if it's a new tent, so you won't be trying to figure out what pole goes in what hole—and which guy lines are missing.

If it's raining hard, try this: Spread the tent on the ground. Quickly lay the rain fly over the tent. Stake out the floor (if needed), then get under the fly yourself if that helps keep you dry. Slip the poles in their holes. Finally, pop it up, with the rain fly still loosely covering the main tent. Then secure the rain fly in place. With a little practice, this procedure should be quick and relatively successful at pitching the tent without getting it overly wet, though it's never much fun.

Another wet-weather strategy is to erect a tarp over your kitchen area, then set up the tent underneath the shelter. Once the tent is pitched, carry it out to the appropriate site. Quickly transfer your dry gear directly from backpack to the tent interior, to minimize getting things wet.

If it's blowing *and* raining, try to wait for a lull in the weather, so you don't soak everything that's supposed to keep you dry. Always stake the windward side first. Otherwise the whole mess will blow into your face. Even if your tent is entirely freestanding, stake it to the ground if there's any doubt of it blowing away. It's no fun watching your dome tent tumble away toward the horizon.

For after-dark tent setup, headlamps make your task easier, but they don't show depth or contour well, because the bulb is on such close parallax with your eyes. To gain a better perspective on ground flatness using a flashlight or headlamp, hold it low to the ground, away from your

When the weather is inclement, you can use a tarp-covered staging area to store gear, set up your tent before moving it to the tent site, and set up the camp kitchen. (Photo: ©Marypat Zitzer)

face, and adjust it until the shadows give you the definition you want. This also works well for after-dark talus walking or following tracks.

When you stake out the guy lines and tighten the rain fly, don't pull too hard at first. You don't want to stretch or strain the fabric. But remember that when the fly gets wet, the weave may open lightly, loosening the fly and forcing you to go outside and tighten the lines. Alas, when it dries again, it will likely shrink some, which could overtighten the lines and stress seams and other weak points. This isn't much of a problem with good modern tents, but if you care about your tent's longevity, don't leave it tight as a drum. Snug is fine.

Make sure that your tent is thoroughly ready for any weather that might appear suddenly while you're strolling on walks from camp or snoring the night away. There's nothing as comforting when sleeping in remote wilderness as having heavy rain wake you from a sound sleep and knowing everything is secured to the maximum extent possible.

Tautline/Rolling Hitch and Trucker's Hitch

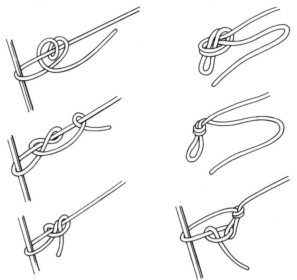

Guying out the tent lines: The tautline or rolling hitch (left) is a sliding knot that works well in most conditions. The trucker's hitch (right) gives you additional leverage when you want to pull a line extra-tight, but be careful not to overtighten because you can weaken tent seams and other stress points.

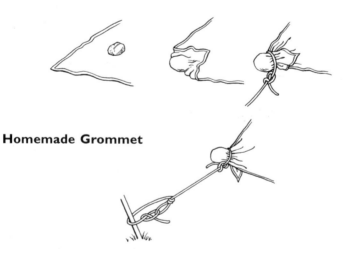

Homemade Grommet

If your tarp does not have grommets or if the grommet has pulled out, you can tie off a stone (or other small object) placed in the corner of the tarp.

Conversely, there are few times so angst-ridden as running around in the stormy dark stashing equipment, or waiting for the first leaks to spring through your rain fly. It is sometimes constructive to look at tent preparation and camp stormproofing as a karmic charm against weather. If you prepare, it won't happen. If you get lazy, the fates will take offense and hammer you.

Tents can absorb a *lot* of solar heat when pitched out in the sun. If you leave your tent erected all day in a hot climate, try to pitch it in the shade; otherwise, it can turn into an oven. Be aware that mosquito netting, particularly tight, no-see-um mesh, restricts air flow, so you might need large mesh panels on a tent in order to move enough air through it in hot, muggy climates. There is an upside to this, because you can use the pronounced infrared heat build-up of a tent interior to dry out clothing and sleeping bags.

Even a cheap department-store tent can survive a heavy mountain rain, but it might require some creativity on your part. Here, a stick is used to prop out the rain fly to keep it separated from the inner tent walls, allowing precipitation and condensation to run off the fly and moisture from inside to escape. (Photo: ©John Harlin)

Set up tents on gravel, sand, and other minimal-impact surfaces to help protect the site from damage. (Photos: ©Alan Kesselheim)

Low-High Venting

Air warms and rises from high end of tent.

Cold air enters low, usually near feet.

Warm, humid air climbs up and out, creating a self-perpetuating draft that clears the tent of condensation and odors.

▲ ▲ ▲

Preparing Your Tent for Sleep and Storm

Be sure to seam-seal your tent before the trip. Allow 24 hours for seam-sealer to dry, and then give it an overnight sprinkler test. Check for leaks. Dry it and fix leaks. Allow another 24 hours for seam-sealer to dry. Once you're in the backcountry, follow these steps:

- Pitch it taut and stake it down well.
- Tension the rain fly so it doesn't touch the interior canopy.
- Leave enough ventilation so that the tent interior stays dry and fresh.
- Protect your sleeping bag against condensation from the tent floor.
- Orient the tent so the door is on the lee side (except in bug country).
- Don't leave your tent set up without staking it down.

Under the Stars

If the weather looks auspicious, and the bug, bear, or wind blast potential is suitably low, don't hesitate to sleep out under the stars. Most of us rarely view the night sky without the glare of city lights, and it's stunning to see just how many stars and meteors are really up there. In northern latitudes during the cooler months, the aurora borealis, or northern lights, are an awe-inspiring reason to sleep out, with their shimmering curtains of emerald, pink, and white.

In tick, mosquito, and blackfly country, tentless slumber is probably not a smart option. In some heavy grizzly country, it's probably not a good idea to sleep outside simply because that's what moose calves and deer fawns do, and they're both food sources. In windy deserts, ground blizzards of sand can be pretty harsh, and often it's more expedient to shelter in a tent rather than endure the grit.

When sleeping in the open, pick a good view and a place sheltered from ground-level wind gusts that might blow leaves and dust in your face. Make sure, however, that you have contingency plans. Arrange a place to scurry to if the weather turns sour (under the cook tarp, in someone's tent, beneath a canoe) and keep a flashlight handy to find the emergency exit.

The halfway house between sleeping out and in the enclosed confines of a tent is to pitch an open-ended tarp. A simple A-frame setup between two trees is an effective shelter and grants much of the quality of sleeping under the stars. The major drawback, of course, is your vulnerability to bugs.

Stowing Bedroll and Gear

After the tent is pitched, lay out your pad and sleeping bag. If you use a self-inflating pad, open the valve; fluff up your sleeping bag on top of your pad, allowing the insulation in both bag and pad to rise to maximum efficiency by the time you turn in. Don't leave clothes or sleeping bags lying outside in windy conditions, or if dew and frost are forming from evening's cooling temperatures.

Before it gets dark, gather what you'll want near at hand during the night, then put it in the pocket on your side of the tent. If it's wet outside, you'll likely want to keep a bandanna or one of those new synthetic quick-dry backpacker's towels near the door to clean up puddles. Dirty socks work okay, too.

THE CAMP KITCHEN

After getting into dry clothes, rehydrating, pitching your tent, and stowing your bedroll and gear, your next priority is eating. According to sports nutritionists, your body is most efficient at digesting food and storing its energy during the first 45 minutes after hard exercise. So stay warm, drink, and eat. It's probably best to start with something light and restorative. Snack on something that doesn't require cooking, and then go about setting up your camp kitchen.

Locate your kitchen (and tent door areas) carefully, because that's where you'll trample the most. The area immediately around your stove or campfire should be a very durable surface devoid of flower patches, moss beds, lichens, and cryptogamic soils. The kitchen should also be near enough for convenience; in bear country, cook and eat at least 100 feet from your sleeping camp, to minimize attractant scents. Your kitchen should be wind-sheltered, so lighting stoves and lanterns can proceed smoothly. It should be reasonably sunny and warm, because you'll probably spend a lot of time there during the cooler periods of morning and evening. Make sure a good site for waste-water disposal (i.e., mineral soil, preferably without vegetation, and at least 200 feet from water) is close at hand. You'll also want a food-hanging tree nearby.

Stoves vs. Fires

There is no actual physiological need for hot food and drinks unless you're hypothermic, but even the most ascetic wilderness traveler quickly discovers that dried or dehydrated foods weigh less, store longer, and taste better than the equivalent caloric quantity of gulp-ready "finger snacks." For those reasons, you'll want to cook most of your backcountry meals, particularly breakfast and dinner.

Campfires were once thought to be indispensable to the outdoor experience, but their impacts have become unacceptable in most wilderness areas: the number of users is outstripping available firewood; campfire sites are unsightly; and fires have a high risk for starting wildfires. In certain environments such as gravelly desert soils and temperate deciduous forests with high regrowth rates, campfires can be built responsibly using existing fire sites, pit fires in mineral soil, metal fire pans, or mylar fire blankets. However, according to extensive research conducted by recreational ecologists connected with the Leave No Trace program, avoiding a campfire is perhaps the single most important thing a wilderness traveler can do to decrease site impact. (For specific information on low-impact camping and fire-building techniques, contact the Leave No Trace hotline at 800-332-4100.)

On many public lands, including national parks, backcountry fires are specifically prohibited. In other national forest and Bureau of Land Management areas, fires are regularly forbidden during times of high wildfire danger. Before visiting an area, make sure to find out what restrictions are currently in effect.

If you're smart, you've already brought enough clothes to stay warm without a fire. If you're particularly chilled, try a hot water bottle nestled under your clothes. If you want light, consider using a small lantern; butane lanterns don't weigh much and they start instantly.

If, in spite of all that, you simply must have a campfire (and it's legal), then choose a campsite with a pre-existing fire scar. If there are multiple scars or rings, pick and use the most logical one, while dismantling and scattering the other rings in order to avoid the proliferation of multiple, unnecessary charred sites.

Sweep the surrounding area of flammable debris before lighting your fire. There is no need to build a ring of stones and there will be less impact if you do not. Check around your campfire area for dry undergrowth, grasses, or mossy, peatlike soils; avoid these. Also make sure that fire conditions aren't so hazardous that you'll start a conflagration. Be extra cautious during hot, dry, windy periods, when wildfires may be a striking side effect of your primal longing to combust cellulose.

▲ ▲ ▲

Reasons Not to Use a Fire

- They're a pain to cook over.
- They blacken pots and pans and create a lot of smoke.
- They send out sparks, which can melt holes in all your nylon gear and clothing.
- They require a lot of time and attention; you have to gather wood, start the fire, and keep the fire going.
- They may be prohibited (check with land managers to make sure restrictions aren't in effect).
- They may burn up precious decaying wood important to the local ecology (especially in subalpine and desert areas).
- They require campers to scrounge the camp area for wood, thus grooming it to something less natural-looking.
- They can start wildfires.

The good news is that portable backpacking stoves are a much more convenient and effective method of cooking than campfires. A modern camp stove will have most meals cooked and ready within 10 to 15 minutes of start-up. A compact stove and two quarts of white gas (about 5 pounds total) will typically keep a party of two in hot food for two weeks on the trail. The speed, convenience, and flame control of a stove is more than enough to offset the added weight.

To take best advantage of a camp stove, use a good windscreen that shelters the flame from breezes that can double your fuel consumption and cooking times. Look for a flat, heat-resistant surface where you won't light the underlying vegetation on fire.

Stove Operation Tips for Specific Models

The Mountain Safety Research (MSR) Whisperlite is easily the backcountry camp stove of choice in North America, mostly due to its reasonable price and year-round performance. It does have a well-deserved reputation for clogging. You can minimize but not stop this clogging by making sure you don't overprime the stove and, during shut down, blow the flame out as soon as possible. Let spewing vapors clear the jet, rather than allowing a small, yellow flame to linger, creating soot that rears its ugly head during the next start-up.

The more expensive MSR XGK is noisier than the Whisperlite but clogs much less often, due to its roarer burner design and thicker fuel supply tube. The same priming and shut-down cautions apply. However, with continuous use, XGKs can develop a weak flame that neither pumping nor cleaning restores. This is due to the stove's sheer heat output, which tends to melt the welded ball at the end of the cable running through the fuel tube, where it sits just under the burner. If you've cleaned your XGK stove and fuel tube, cleared the jet, and still experience weak performance, correct the problem as follows:

First, remove the flame spreader and carefully unscrew the fuel jet (you can mar the soft brass of the burner and jet threads if you're not careful, creating flame leakage around the jet, so handle your screwdriver very gently). Then remove the fuel tube cable using the tool provided with the stove. Grind the burner end of the fuel cable against a file, rock, or piece of sandpaper, roughing up the round melted ball at the cable's burner end. Do not try to grind the ball away; merely reduce its size and rough it up. Reinsert the cable in the tube, attach the fuel bottle, then

Camp stoves come in two varieties, those with the tank underneath the stove and those with the tank (generally the fuel bottle) to the side. (Photo: ©Marypat Zitzer)

allow some fuel to run through the tube, clearing out soot, dust, and debris that may have dislodged during cable removal. Then carefully replace the burner jet and flame spreader. Refire the stove. Full performance should be restored. You'll probably need to repeat this procedure about every 10 field days, and when you remove the cable again, you'll notice the melted ball has grown back to its original size and smoothness.

Peak 1 Feather and Multi-fuel models are tank-under stoves justifiably renowned for their high heat output and ability to simmer well, but they do not work well in winter. Peak 1 tank-unders are also notorious for transitory problems. Sometimes they work superbly, while the next trip they may clog without any obvious cause. All Peak 1 stoves love to be pumped, so if heat output is merely weak, pump away. Make sure the pump cup is lubricated with oil, and replace it if it's worn.

The Optimus 8R and Svea 123 R are time-tested classics, basically unchanged since the 1950s. Both models require a practiced touch when priming, because priming not only preheats the brass stem that provides fuel to the burner, but also pressurizes the tank. For easier priming and better cold-weather performance, use the optional fuel tank pump, which helps greatly with priming and pressurization.

Stove Maintenance on the Trail

Your particular model of camp stove may be finicky or it may be a die-hard, but all stoves benefit from careful handling in the backcountry. To avoid bending parts or cracking fuel tubes, pack your stove carefully rather than cramming it into your load like clothing. Keep your stove clean.

Maintain or replace rubber gaskets, particularly fuel bottle, fuel tank, and fuel tube seals, which can cause fires if they degrade. Leather or plastic pump cups that slide up and down in fuel-tank pressurization pumps need to be kept flexible and lubricated by an occasional cleaning and the application of oil, silicone, or—in the absence of appropriate materials—lip balm. Keep repair parts with your stove. Most manufacturers offer a standard kit that contains the most commonly needed parts. Periodically clean the fuel jet (sometimes called the "nipple"). Commercially available cleaners, made of thin, stiff wire, are available for most stoves. If you can't obtain them, toothbrush bristles will also work.

Cooking in a Tent

The rule about cooking in your tent is: don't. In three-season camping, this rule typically isn't too hard to follow, but heavy rain, stiff wind, and winter temperatures pose a dilemma for those trained to the no-stoves-in-tents mantra. When weather forces the issue, retreat under a tarp first (assuming you've got one) and continue cooking there. If you don't have a tarp or the wind's too much, then cook in the floorless vestibule of your tent, but prime the stove outside, because that's when flame flare-ups are worst.

If your tent doesn't have a floorless vestibule, you're best off setting the stove at arm's length outside the tent door and unzipping the door for stirring and flame adjustments. Don't take the stove inside your living space unless forced to by weather, and then be extra cautious of fuel spills or tent floor melt-throughs. Always prime your stove outside, and wait until flaring flames die down before moving the stove under cover. In the tent, use a piece of insulating material such as a foam sleeping pad, a commercially made stove base, or a specially cut chunk of floor tile (even an old license plate helps) to keep the hot stove burner from melting through your tent's floor. Be careful when using some butane canister stoves where the fuel cartridge attaches to the burner unit with a long, flexible tube, because the stove flame may flare quite high if the canister is tipped on its side. Experienced campers—even ones who know their stove intimately—have all had scary, weird flare-ups at least once in their careers. So beware.

You shouldn't cook inside a tent because stove flare-ups are common, especially with white-gas models, but if you must, be sure to light the stove outside and cook next to the partially open door. (Photo: ©John Harlin)

When cooking from the tent on a drizzly day, place the stove on a rock base to prevent tipping and set it up outside the tent to preclude an in-tent fire. (Photo: ©Alan Kesselheim)

If you do cook inside your tent, as many thousands of campers have, understand the true dangers—the biggest of which is carbon monoxide poisoning. If your tent is sealed up, you could unknowingly be breathing carbon monoxide, a poisonous but odorless gas. Carbon monoxide will first give you a headache, then put you to sleep, and finally kill you. So if you cook inside (or use a lantern or any type of heater), ventilate the tent.

▲ ▲ ▲

Hot Tips for Living with Your Stove

Test-fire any new camp stove at home before relying on it in the field. Problems in the backyard can be easily resolved; problems in the field can mean disaster.

- Pack your stove and fuel carefully in a side pocket, in a padded bag, or in a special stove case, away from food or clothing.
- Carry jet-cleaning needles taped to your stove or fuel bottle, and keep key spare parts in the burner stuff sack. Stove maintenance is generally simple: Learn to recognize problems and make repairs before they're necessary.
- Check the fuel for water or sediment before filling a gas or kerosene stove. Fuel sometimes develops condensation during storage, particularly in partially full containers. Use a filter funnel to keep detritus from clogging fuel lines.
- Use a stove base when cooking on snow, uneven ground, or, in emergencies, on tent floors.
- Clean your stove if it won't run at full efficiency, because excessive carbon build-up only worsens the situation.
- Cover pots with a tight-fitting lid and use a windscreen to increase efficiency. An unprotected burner in moderate wind may take twice as long to boil a quart of water. A full wraparound windscreen is most effective, but make sure it isn't reflecting excessive heat onto the gas tank.
- Cook with a blackened pot, because it heats faster than a reflective, silvery one. Blacken the pot with spray-on stovepipe paint. A heat exchanger (such as the model available from MSR) further decreases boiling times and fuel consumption rates, which become logistically important on long treks.
- Always carry extra fuel because even the best stoves won't run on empty.

A heat exchanger traps warm air from the stove next to the pot and transfers considerably more heat than would be possible without the exchanger, saving its weight in fuel within a few days of use.
(Photo: Jeff Scher ©ERG)

Purifying Water

No matter how thirsty you are once you've located water, and no matter how pristine its appearance, it is wise to purify it. How wise? In a recent examination of 10,000 American streams, not one was found without *Giardia lamblia*—a parasite deposited into the water through an infected animal's feces. (Giardiasis was once known as "beaver fever," though other animals, including humans, are also carriers.) Ingest this protozoan and you'll be fine for 5 to 7 days, but then diarrhea strikes and stays for a week or longer. Some of the other symptoms of giardiasis are abdominal cramps, weight loss, and fatigue. Not a single tested stream in all Colorado, for that matter, was found free of the parasite.

Unfortunately, it gets worse: Giardia is not the only parasite out there. Cryptosporidium brings on symptoms very similar to Giardia, while the fellow-protozoan *Entamoeba histolytica* causes amoebic dysentery. And then there are the bacteria (you've probably heard of shigella, which causes dysentery, and *Salmonella typhosa*, which brings on typhoid) and viruses (hepatitis A and E, Norwalk virus, rotavirus . . .), all before you get to the unsightly stuff that can actually be seen with the naked eye, floating in or swimming about in the water you're planning to imbibe. Ugh.

Boiling. But there are ways to kill these critters. The first method, fatal to all the microorganisms, is boiling. The good news is that the old rule about having to boil water for 10 minutes, plus 1 minute for every 1,000 feet of elevation, is incorrect. Bringing the water to a boil—period—kills the nasty protozoans and bacteria. The Center for Disease Control in Atlanta suggests boiling for 3 minutes to be sure about the viruses. Nevertheless, any amount of boiling is time- and fuel-consuming.

Iodine treatment has long been a common method of purification. Used in either liquid or tablet form, iodine's drawbacks were once just the time you had to wait for the killer chemical to do its work (10 to 30 minutes, depending upon the murkiness and temperature of the water), the color it gave to the water (that of a murky raspberry tea), and the taste. Although lime juice and other flavored drinks can counteract the taste, there is now an additional treatment (in the form of lightweight pills) that will also do the trick. While it is suggested that iodine-treated water should not be drunk for longer than three months at a stretch, nor drunk at all by women who are pregnant or by people with thyroid

conditions, iodine was (past tense) the safest, surest, least expensive, and most convenient purifier for the greatest number of folks hitting the backcountry. Until, that is, the rise of that difficult-to-kill "crypto" (Cryptosporidium). This protozoan is equipped with a shell sufficiently strong to laugh at the effects of iodine. More's the pity, for now you either have to boil water or use a water filter.

Water filter. And just to put another twist to the problem, while all the major brands of portable lightweight water filters will strain out the relatively large protozoans and bacteria, viruses—the tiniest of the three categories of organisms—will sail on through. They must be boiled away, or knocked dead with iodine. Some water filters come equipped with an

A water purifier at work in the wilds. (Photo: ©Dennis Coello)

Opposite page: Water may look clean, but always treat it before drinking. (Photo: ©Dennis Coello)

iodine chamber, to guarantee full protection. Or you can add it to the water you've just filtered. Avoid turbid, silt-laden water, because it quickly clogs most backcountry filters and you'll have to backwash or clean the filter, or replace the cartridge altogether. If you must use murky water, strain it through something (cheesecloth is great) to capture the large chunks. You can also gather it in a pot, then let the particulates settle out before filtering the clear remainder. If you have the option, let water sit for an hour or two or even overnight.

Making it palatable. The taste of backcountry water varies widely, and not all wilderness water is delightful. In the desert, dissolved minerals can make for decidedly unpalatable drinking. In autumn deciduous forests' decaying leaves can impart a musty flavor. You can always make water taste better by boiling it, then letting the sediment settle before drawing off the clarified water and using that. Citrus tablets, activated-charcoal after-filters, coffees, teas, and powdered drink mixes also help. Even if the local water fails the gourmet test, chug it down, because you must rehydrate.

▲ ▲ ▲

Dealing with Water

- Filter, boil, or purify all water.
- Drink plenty to rehydrate.
- Have a full bottle available at bedtime and when leaving camp in the morning.
- Let turbid water settle out its sediment before filtering or using.
- Use a large-volume water bag for your camp supply, to minimize trips.
- Boil poor-tasting water, settle sediments, then pour off clarified water for use.
- Use citrus tablets or powdered drink mixes to help counteract poor water taste.
- Filter waste water through a strainer to remove particulates; pack those out with garbage.
- Pour waste water 200 feet away from water sources, on mineral soil if possible, avoiding plants.

Camp Cuisine

The water's gathered. Your stoves are up and running. Hot drinks are cooking, and you've secured your camp to the degree desirable. So pull up a seat, it's time to eat. On the trail, food is a larger-than-life subject, far more than mere calories to keep the body running. Camp food can also be a motivator in trying times, a social event, a divine hedonistic experience, an artistic creation. (It can also be an opportunity for mayhem!) A detailed discussion of camp cuisine is a topic too large for this book, so check out one of the many books or articles on the subject if you need ideas.

Whether or not the stove is fired up, the camp kitchen is generally the place where people gather. (Photo: ©Marypat Zitzer)

SANITATION

If there is one point in this chapter where we grapple with the truly nitty-gritty, it is right here. Pee, poop, food slops, gray water, garbage—hard to get much earthier than that!

At home, our trash is picked up and our human wastes are flushed away. Whole industries are devoted to keeping these nasty and private necessities out of view and out of mind. In camp, however, we must deal with wastes in a way that keeps us clean and healthy, while ensuring the continued purity of the backcountry.

The overall goals of camp sanitation are:

- Maintain the integrity of the environment, especially the water quality and vegetation.
- Avoid attracting wildlife.
- Keep a clean and healthy campsite, leaving little sign of your passing.
- Encourage the rapid decomposition of any wastes left behind.

Garbage

The rule of thumb is to pack out everything you brought in. "Pack it out" includes leftover food, plastic bags, cans, unburned matches, used toilet paper, candy wrappers . . . everything. (The only exception, in most cases, is bodily wastes.) Bring heavy-gauge plastic bags to carry out food scraps. Before leaving camp, take a final pass over the ground, looking for the small, elusive bits of trash like twist ties, rubber bands, matchsticks, and dental floss.

Sanitary napkins or tampons should be bagged and carried out, along with used toilet paper. Toilet paper can be completely burned in a hot fire (if building a fire is legal and appropriate). After burning paper trash, stir the coals to make sure everything has been consumed and that there aren't any errant bits lurking in the charcoal.

Gray Water, Soap, and Toothpaste

Excess cooking water and dishwater should be drained at least 200 feet from a stream or lake and screened to avoid leaving food scraps on the ground that will attract flies and wildlife. A lightweight mesh screen (available at discount stores) serves this purpose well and takes up little space in a pack. Small food scraps can then be added to the trash bag. Try to find soil free of vegetation when dumping gray water, especially if the water is soapy or greasy.

On camping trips with your family or small groups whose germs you are confident of, consider not using soap to wash with. Soap is a major culprit in degrading water and damaging vegetation. Hot water combined with a scrubby or sand does a passable job on dishes unless there is a lot of grease. With larger groups and tougher cleaning jobs, choose a soap brand that is phosphate free, and make sure to dispose of it at least 200 feet from the nearest water.

When bathing, either dip in a stream or lake without using soap or wash with soap by taking water in a cook pot at least 200 feet from the nearest water. Instead of using soap to wash clothes, simply rinse them out thoroughly or wait till you get home.

Toothpaste odors attract animals, and their residue can damage plant life. Either go without toothpaste in the backcountry (the brush is the important thing!), or use brands without mint or flavoring. Spit into a shallow scrape of bare ground, rinse the spot with water, and cover lightly with dirt. Some people like to spray their toothpaste in a forceful spit that spreads the rinse in a fine mist.

Human Waste

Protection of water quality is the most important goal of sanitary waste disposal. Contamination of rivers and lakes is a widespread and growing problem.

Peeing in the outdoors is relatively harmless if you are disease-free. In pristine sites, a healthy human's urine is sterile and has no more impact than that of passing wildlife. In camps that are more heavily used, however, it is best to pee at least 100 feet from camp and to avoid urinating on vegetation that might be harmed or defoliated by animals hungry for salts. Mineral soil or bare rock are the ideal targets.

Human feces are more problematic. In truly wild areas, we can poop in much the same way as the animals do, either digging shallow "cat holes" or leaving our solid wastes on the ground, open to rapid decomposition by air, sunlight, and moisture. Feces are, however, carriers of disease and pathogens, and in camps that are more regularly used, or where we stay for more than a few days, their sanitary disposal is critical. Some areas (heavily used river corridors, for instance, or fragile beaches) require users to pack their poop out or use portable toilets (see chapter 2, Canoeing, Kayaking, and Rafting).

The old latrine method has fallen out of favor, because it disturbs a relatively large area, concentrates wastes in a deep hole that retards decomposition, and is difficult to cover up adequately. Latrines are really only viable for long stays with a large group. They should be at least 1 foot deep and should be covered over again when filled within 4 or 5 inches of the top.

Cat holes. More often, the approved technique involves digging small, single-use cat holes at least 200 feet from water sources. These holes should be about 4 inches square and 4 to 6 inches deep. When the camper finishes, cover the hole (without leaving toilet paper) and camouflage the ground.

Surface disposal. This method has more recently found advocates, because of the rapid decomposition of feces left in the open air. The drawbacks are that disease can spread relatively easily and, in high-use areas, the wastes are both dangerous and unsightly. In fact, surface disposal is illegal in much of the backcountry. In remote, little-traveled regions (parts of the Far North, for instance), surface disposal is appropriate well off trails and at least 200 feet from water. If possible, smear feces with a stick or rock to increase exposure to the elements and encourage rapid breakdown.

Toilet paper. In terms of its longevity and unsightliness, toilet paper is a bigger backcountry problem than bodily wastes. Used toilet paper scattered in the bushes at an otherwise beautiful campsite is enough to make most of us want to turn tail and move on. Fact is, you can do without toilet paper in most instances. Smooth rocks, broad leaves, or a small handful of snow are workable substitutes, once you get in the habit, and you aren't then left to deal with disgusting litter. Be sure to wash hands well afterward. If toilet paper is a must, be sure to use an unscented brand, use as little as possible, and pack it out along with other garbage. You can also burn it if there is a safe and responsible site for a fire and you can burn it completely in a hot blaze.

SHUTTING DOWN FOR THE DAY

With your basic needs of shelter, clothing, and food provided for, and matters of sanitation taken care of, it's time to kick back and savor the setting and companionship of the outdoors. There is an art to this, and it's a subtle yet important one. Particularly during the cooler seasons, when nights are longer, much of any wilderness trekker's time is spent in a dark camp, and occupying one's time pleasantly should be a priority. Backpack camping is, after all, recreation.

Evening Activities

Some groups simply wish to bundle up and watch the heavens, or scribble in diaries by candlelight. Others break out guitars and playing cards, whiskey and cigars, massage oil and wine glasses, nature guides and books of poetry. With larger groups, one or two bright camp lanterns greatly help with socializing and camp functions, even if you've got a fire going. The lightweight butane/propane lanterns are particularly nice for smaller groups and winter camping, because they weigh little (the burner heads can be switched back and forth between stove and lantern), provide good light, have modest fuel requirements, and burn clean enough to be used as a tent heater.

While companionship is a true wilderness pleasure, don't forget to step outside the social circle occasionally and walk away from camp to sample the silence of the wilderness. It's easy to overlook moments of stunning natural beauty when you're staring into coals or grousing with your buddies about troubles back home. To see full moons, fog on a moonlit lake, and shooting stars, or to hear the roar of brisk winds being combed by a million pine needles, take a moment and stand someplace quiet. Those profoundly still moments are the ones you'll remember years hence.

Strolls. Rather than considering yourself stranded by the bound-aries of your camp, consider taking an evening stroll. Evening is one of the day's best times for beautiful sky colors or wildlife watching. You're way out there. You've hiked a long time during the day. Your early hours in camp were probably relatively quiet, and often the resident animals have resumed their nearby foraging. By walking quietly away from your backcountry homestead, you can become a participant in the daily pat-terns of these amazing places, while loosening up hard-worked muscles as a transition toward sleep.

Stretching. Another refreshing diversion is to spend some time stretching. Backpacking's good for your aerobic capacity, leg muscle

Stretching helps you relax in the evening and loosens stiff, tired muscles at the end of a day. (Photo: ©Jeff Scher)

strengthening, and general conditioning, but it does nothing for flexibility or skeletal alignment. In other words, backpacking, while restorative, is not an athletic antidote for stiff, office-chair back problems. Trail muscles get sore. Eventually, strained muscles quit doing their full work, which causes tendons to take over. Because tendons are much less flexible than muscles, this can progress to disabling tendonitis, if you let significant pain go unmitigated.

Take 15 minutes or a half hour to lay out your pad on some flat and scenic site and do stretches to loosen up your legs and lower back. Once you convince your tired self to begin, stretching becomes a deliriously sensual experience, and it will help you avoid the stress injuries brought on by sleeping bag contortions and the unaccustomed load weight of pack or canoes.

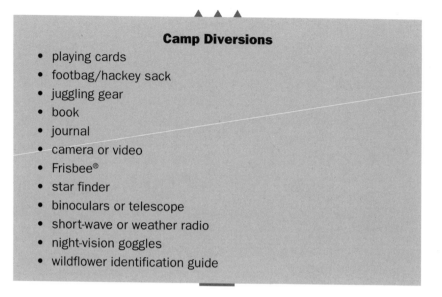

▲ ▲ ▲

Camp Diversions

- playing cards
- footbag/hackey sack
- juggling gear
- book
- journal
- camera or video
- Frisbee®
- star finder
- binoculars or telescope
- short-wave or weather radio
- night-vision goggles
- wildflower identification guide

Securing Camp

Eventually your conversational pauses lengthen, your legs feel heavy, and your head nods forward. It's time to quit. Rest your body. Enjoy the deep sleep that comes from a snug bed in the cool, crisp air. But first you've got to batten down camp against potential weather, pick up your kitchen, consolidate your gear, store everything in weatherproof, easy-to-locate fashion. Secure key items so that even if a typhoon blew through you'd still have your shoes, rain shell, compass, matches, et cetera.

Tarps strung over the kitchen area should be pulled down and de-rigged if winds or rain-loading might collapse them overnight. Drying clothes should be secured against rain, or stored inside if weather threatens. Your pack should be strapped up tight to shed rain and strung in a tree or some other secure location, such as in the tent vestibule, if there's room. Tent vestibules are great for keeping dirty and wet stuff secure, while still keeping it all out of your living space proper. Probe the corners of your camp with a light, because small things tend to get missed in the dark.

Water. In winter, protect liquids against overnight freezing. You can let pans of water freeze up pretty well, because the ice expands upward rather than splitting the pot. But letting water bottles freeze splits them. Wide-mouth bottles are easier to get liquids from when partially frozen, but if overnight temperatures fall significantly below 32 degrees Fahrenheit, consider protecting your water. You can store drinking water in the foot of your bag, but a cold water bottle will chill you. Conversely, you can boil up your water and store it as a toasty hot water bottle, perfect for pumping heat into chilled toes.

Critter-proofing. The most problematic aspect of the evening routine (especially in well-used sites) is what to do with your food. In many established and managed campsites, there are bear-box containers or food-hanging setups to secure the food bag from the raids of bears, raccoons, skunks, and other varmints. Barring that, there are several steps you can take, listed here in ascending order of rigor:

1. Stow the food and other gear at a distance from the tents (to minimize potential animal/people encounters) in tightly sealed containers (double bags, plastic barrels with screw tops, boxes with gasket seals, et cetera).
2. Strategically place fresh mothballs around the food packs to discourage animals (these actually seem to work!).
3. Hang the food bag from a branch so it is roughly 4 feet from the trunk and 8 feet from the ground.
4. A tin can lid with a hole drilled through it (tuna can or larger), slipped halfway down a hanging cord and held in place by a knot, foils most rodents.
5. Create your own food-hanging pulley system with ropes, making sure your food bag is at least 8 feet off the ground and 4 feet from the nearest tree trunk or weight-bearing branch.

Specially designed bear bags have ready-to-throw cords and weights, making bearproofing simple, and their high cost is probably worthwhile for people who regularly camp in bear country. For most folks, though, coated nylon stuff bags with trash can liners inside suffice to protect food against weather and abrasion. Carry about 50 feet of tent cord or bootlace nylon (or use a rescue throw-bag if you're on the river) for the bear-bag rope.

Trees suitable for hanging food are often scarce, especially in the desert, alpine areas, and tundra, and rigging a foolproof setup can be tricky. Bears are a good deal more agile, acrobatic, and powerful at climbing than humans, so even if you do get the food hung, you may be fated to a sleepless night spent listening to an increasingly frustrated bear trying to get at your food (and more than likely succeeding).

While bear bags are a necessary hassle of traveling in bruin country, there are several strategies to help minimize contact. Rely on clean camping practices as the first line of defense. Leave aromatic foods (like tinned fish snacks) at home. Use relatively odor-free food containers. Avoid staying in the same camp day after day, and make every attempt to avoid camps where obvious bear sign is evident. Avoid activities like

How to Mouse-proof

In a shelter or hut, a tin can lid secured by a knot will prevent most rodents from dining on your food.

Two Methods of Bear-bagging

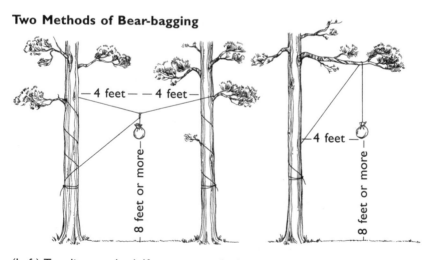

(Left) Two-line method: If you cannot find a tree with a good horizontal limb, string a line between two trees and then use a second line to raise and lower your food with a pulley or carabiner set up on the tightrope. (Right) One-line method: Tie a rock or a small stuff sack with a few rocks in it to the end of your line and throw the line over the tree limb.

Bear bagging is always easier in theory than in practice. (Photo: John Harlin ©ERG)

fishing or hunting, which heavily scent a camp. Even if you take a short hike from camp, secure everything—your food is at risk anytime you aren't immediately around it. The cleaner and more secure your camp, the more carefully and noisily you travel, the less risk you run of an unpleasant ursine encounter.

There should not be any food inside your tent. Candy bars, a bag of trail mix, some dried fruit—all taboo! Food in the tent is an open invitation to animals. In fact, even things like flavored toothpaste are questionable. In bear country, some campers change out of the clothes they had on during dinner and leave them outside to avoid bringing food smells into the tent with them.

As a final precaution in bear land, some adventurers carry a pepper spray canister with convenient holster. Pepper spray is the best bear protection short of a gun (and better than a gun in many circumstances), and it has the overwhelming advantage of not wreaking permanent injury on an animal that was probably attracted through your carelessness.

Settling In

Make sure all your critical gear is rounded up in preparation for the next morning. Your boots should be handy, yet protected from rain or salt-gnawing rodents. A full bottle of water should be close at hand so you can quench your thirst at night, and have a full pot of water ready for morning cooking. Any protective equipment such as bear repellent sprays should be nearby. There's nothing so restful as knowing you're prepared for anything.

Take precautions to keep bugs and sand out as you make your way into the tent for the night. Leave shoes in the vestibule, just outside the door, or in a stuff sack/plastic bag inside the tent. Remember where they are in case of midnight outings! If the bugs are buzzing, make your entrance quickly, zip the door shut immediately, and then hunt down any intruders.

As you undress every night, establish a routine place for your clothes. Some people fold clothes to make a pillow, while others (most often paddlers) bring their own small pillow (inflatable, in-flight style, et cetera). The rest of your clothes could go under the foot of your sleeping bag if extra insulation is a concern, or on top of your clothes bag. Any damp socks, wet bandannas, or other clothing that isn't dry should be draped from a window pocket, hung from a line, or laid out to dry. As you nestle in, you have the option of setting your alarm or not.

To folks who never camp, the thought of bedding down with a ½ inch of foam beneath you seems spartan indeed. But for the camper, fresh from the rigors of exercise and outdoor weather, that same mattress feels like a warm, dry cocoon.

Many folks prefer sleeping naked, but even if you're a pajama camper, don't leave on any of the clothes you've worn during the day. They may feel dry, but residual moisture will wick away your body's heat.

Night light. Your flashlight should be in the tent for nighttime trips and emergencies. You'll want to know where it is at all times. A candle lantern is a pleasant source of evening light for making journal entries, reading, or playing cards. Hang it by a cord from the center of the tent, well away from flammable fabric. A simple candle holder can be fashioned by filling a plastic bag (or empty can) with loose dirt or sand, then pushing the candle firmly into the center. Larger lanterns (especially gas-fueled) are problematic, are overkill, and are dangerous inside a tent.

Ventilation. Air movement is crucial to maintaining a comfortable and dry tent environment. Even in stormy weather, try to keep the door flap and at least one window flap partly open. A closed-up tent is stuffy, hot, and moist, while air flow keeps the atmosphere fresh and minimizes the build-up of condensation over the night hours. It is also important to maintain air space between breathable tent fabric and the waterproof fly. Most tents are designed to insure this, but make sure you rig the fly to facilitate air space.

Adjusting to the outdoors. It often takes a night or two to let your body and mind adjust to sleeping outside the usual, sheltering room. Camping novices especially may have trouble sleeping for a night or two, until they become accustomed to the unusual nighttime setting. Many experienced backpackers also sleep poorly the first night or two of a backpacking trip, until they shed the angst of city living and relax into the slower rhythms of the wilderness. As well, noisy storms and blustery weather, even raucous night animals, can create a subtle anxiety that inhibits sleep, particularly if you're pinned down in a remote location. Fortunately, after a night or two, most folks pass through a threshold of backcountry relaxation, and sleep tends to come pretty easy.

If the storms get loud, consider using earplugs to allow you needed rest. They offer a warm, insulative kind of isolation, and that peaceful core is important to maximizing your rest every evening. You generally sleep more hours on the average backcountry night than at home, due to the early curfew of sundown and darkness, so a bit of restless tossing usually results in more midnight boredom than morning fatigue.

Noise is also a problem when your tent mate is snoring lustily. In such cases, hope for good weather so you can drag your bag out under the stars. If you're pinned inside, roll the offender onto his or her side or stomach; as a last resort, keep nudging the snorer awake all night. Misery loves company.

Group situations. Camping with companions is like a big slumber party, and it's always fun. But you're also sleeping in thin-walled tents that don't stop many sounds. Snoring companions, noisy conversations, and group sing-alongs can occasionally put a damper on your attempts at peaceful sleep. Light sleepers should camp a bit away from the main group. In benign weather, your best solution when caught by late-night parties is to move away from the disturbance. A little distance does wonders for solitude.

When a fairly high density of campers descends on a given region all looking for wilderness solitude, neighboring groups can irritate each other. Land managers term this friction "user conflict," and it can arise between different user groups such as backpackers and motorcyclists, or between parties traveling by the same mode but having dissimilar styles— perhaps a noisy, social group camped near one that's looking for quiet, or one that likes late-night sing-alongs when a nearby group is trying to sleep. It can even entail moderate conversation that ricochets off nearby cliffs and travels a half mile, preventing other campers from sleeping.

There's really only three solutions to such situations. First and easiest, you can move away from the disturbance. Second, you can communicate politely with the offenders, bringing up your objections in nonabrasive style, which may or may not result in a compromise. Third, you can be aware of the impact and noise your own party is generating, to avoid heedlessly annoying your neighbors.

You can also suppress a lot of this friction at its source, which is, after all, the internal attitude of the one being annoyed. Many of us visit the wilderness to lose the tensions of high-pressure modern life. Sometimes, in order to maximize your wilderness enjoyment, you've got to consciously shed all the pent-up angst. It's hard to enjoy the rugged beauty of mountains, quiet sounds of a stream, or piercing scents of a wildflower field if you're spending all your time grousing about other wilderness visitors. Urban mental baggage can be a heavy load to carry. If it's weighing heavily, leave it behind. You'll sleep better.

Staying warm. There are two times during an average night when you might get cold. One is when you first crawl into your sleeping bag for the night. The interior of the bag itself needs to be heated. You might have been chilled from standing outside in evening cold. The immediate discomfort of a cold bag tends to disappear quickly, but sometimes it can take an hour or so before you're up to temperature for the rest of the night. The solution is to stay warm and fed upon arriving in camp, choose a sleeping bag for the coldest duty you expect to use, and change into dry sleeping clothes. Should you need more insulation than your sleeping bag provides, additional dry clothing layers, particularly on the torso and head, will help you warm up.

The other time you may easily become chilled is just before dawn, when nighttime temperatures are normally at their lowest and you've probably been asleep for some time, so your body-heat output is also low. The best ways to meet this metabolic challenge are to choose a sleeping bag that's warm enough, keep spare clothing readily at hand, and (in places were marauding wildlife isn't an issue) have a few high-energy snacks handy to provide fuel for your body's warming fires.

Getting up in the night. There are usually two reasons to go out of the tent during the night. The first is to heed nature's call. This is when knowing where you left the flashlight and your shoes comes in. Take care not to rouse your tent mates, and zip the door behind you! If a storm is pounding or the bugs are intolerable, you may want to resort to a pee bottle system whereby you urinate into a clearly designated wide-mouth container. The logistics of this maneuver are, as you might imagine, somewhat delicate and prone to comical mishap.

The second reason to venture out is to attach the rain fly you confidently left off under clear evening skies. Hours later, to your surprise and consternation, you wake to the patter of rain on your unprotected tent canopy. If you take the risk of going flyless, make sure you leave the rain fly and necessary stakes accessible, and be familiar enough with their installation so that you can manage it largely by feel in the dark.

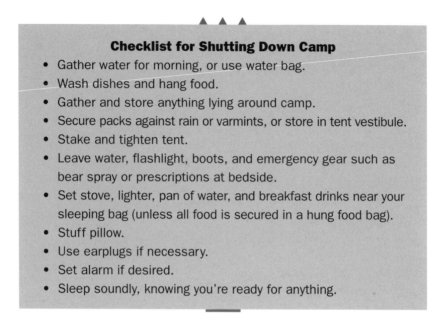

Checklist for Shutting Down Camp

- Gather water for morning, or use water bag.
- Wash dishes and hang food.
- Gather and store anything lying around camp.
- Secure packs against rain or varmints, or store in tent vestibule.
- Stake and tighten tent.
- Leave water, flashlight, boots, and emergency gear such as bear spray or prescriptions at bedside.
- Set stove, lighter, pan of water, and breakfast drinks near your sleeping bag (unless all food is secured in a hung food bag).
- Stuff pillow.
- Use earplugs if necessary.
- Set alarm if desired.
- Sleep soundly, knowing you're ready for anything.

BREAKING CAMP

Morning and sunrise are much more than a tape of evening played in reverse. In the taste of its air, the colors of the sky, and the often dubious pleasure of awakening, mornings are a far cry from the genteel charms of evening. At night you slowly descend into a secure, snug, cocoonlike state. In the morning, you emerge again into the world, and it's anybody's guess as far as weather conditions. You could rise to warm sunshine or blustery rain.

If you've secured and organized your camp prior to retiring, all this morning confusion goes much easier, because your clothes and shoes and stove are all ready. Morning oatmeal and drinks, fixed from your sleeping bag and eaten in bed, can give you a snug and solid start on the earliest day. If you've been choosy in your campsites, you might even have the sun's early rays baking you warmer as you curl around the java. Or perhaps you chose a fine view and have the camera tripod already set up next to your bed, so you can snap off a dawn shot and go back to sleep.

Getting Breakfast

There are those fortunate individuals who can go from "zero to sixty" immediately upon awakening. But the neurons of most mortal humans tend to report for duty one at a time, and for most people, IQ is not maximized until well after caffeine ingestion. Groups with mixed tastes—tea, hot chocolate, Postum, coffee—have to compromise. Boil up a pot of water and let everyone pour their beverage of choice. Regardless what your morning beverage is, down plenty of drinks at breakfast.

Coffee. If the entire group is in agreement in its need for java, a pot of cowboy coffee is the easiest way to accommodate. Just dump four or five handsful of grounds in a pot of cold water, bring to a rolling boil, and remove from the heat. Pour in a half cup of cold water to settle the grounds, and you're all set. One-cup coffee filter cones that don't require paper inserts (or can take reusable cloth filters) allow you to enjoy your single cup of coffee if no one else is interested. An amazing assortment of coffee gadgetry has made its way onto the camping scene, so you can get as fanatic as you like. Camp-stove espresso units, coffee bags (tea bags full of coffee grounds), compact hand-crank coffee bean grinders, cappuccino condiment kits, and various flavor packets are all available to serve the most demanding caffeine connoisseurs.

Espresso, anyone? This model is made for trail use. (Photo: ©Marypat Zitzer)

Preparing for the Day's Journey

While you're eating and dressing around breakfast, start feeding all your stuff into the day's pack. Begin by tearing down your sleeping bag and tent setup, because these store best in the bottom of your pack anyway. In dry weather, you can leave your sleeping pad out and use it like a table on which to sort smaller items. In rainy weather take the tarp and tent down last, so everything else is sheltered in your backpack by the time you "strike canvas." This works out well because these will be the first items you'll want upon arrival at the evening's campsite, but it makes accessing other day gear harder. As you keep feeding stuff into the backpack, pile on the sleeping gear, your extra food, your clothing, then kitchen items.

Camp breaking also involves preparation for your day's ensuing journey. Just as you went to bed with a full water bottle and everything prepared, so you should leave camp with midmorning snacks ready for on-the-move eating, and travel items like map, compass, sunglasses, sunscreen, blister remedies, binoculars, cameras, and extra clothing for your brief rest stops all ready at hand. Carry enough water and handy snacks to get you through to lunch before refilling.

Taking Down the Tent

Because wet tents weigh more, your major need is to dry it as thoroughly as possible before stuffing it in your pack. When you remove the fly, have your partner take the far end, then hold it vertically and shake it violently side to side. This will dislodge the great majority of the moisture. Then, if it's a dry morning, drape the fly over a bush with the wettest side facing the sun. The tent floor will almost always be damp, so be sure to dismantle the tent early (assuming it's not raining) and drape it bottom-out until you're ready to load your pack. If you have a freestanding tent, leave the door open and simply tip the tent bottom side up until it dries.

The great debate is whether to stuff your tent or roll it, and if you roll it, whether to roll it around your tent poles or keep them separate. The concern about rolling has to do with creasing the coated pieces (floor and fly) in the same place, over and over, until the coating cracks. It's also a pain to roll a tent on wet sand, mud, or snow. Stuffing circumvents these problems. The concern about rolling the tent around the poles is whether their sharp or burred ends might poke the tent fabric. Another reason for carrying the poles separately is that the weight can be divided between partners and, divided into two bundles, the tent usually fits better into a pack.

If it's raining, you might choose to simply collapse the whole affair, leaving the rain fly on top. Then quickly stuff the tent into its sack (all this taking place under the flat rain fly). Finally, shake out the rain fly as described above and stuff it into a separate sack. Savvy outdoorspeople differ in their approaches, so choose the one that makes sense to you.

Pulling Apart Camp

By the time you're finished breaking down camp and stowing items for logical access, you'll have finished eating and drinking, your pack will be nearly packed, and you'll be lacing your boots and stripping down for the day's exercise. As soon as the stove burner's cool, you're outta there. And everything's loaded into your pack in perfect sequence for arriving in your next backpack campsite. Then it's time for a quick check of your campsite to avoid leaving any trace of your presence.

Take off.

North shore of Lake Superior (Photo: ©Alan Kesselheim)

CHAPTER 2

CANOEING, KAYAKING, AND RAFTING

—

At Home by the Water's Edge

Alan Kesselheim

EVEN THOUGH IT IS LATE AFTERNOON, we load the canoe and start paddling as soon as the wind dies. For a day and a half, we have been held windbound in a dreary campsite, waiting for a break, so when we finally leave it feels like a liberation.

At first the waves on the big lake are still choppy and threatening, but within a mile they broaden and flatten out. For another mile there are gentle, steady swells, like a memory of the winds that lathered up the water. Then the lake goes flat in the evening light. The canoe draws a straight furrow across this liquid field, and we gather up the distance with an appetite fueled by the pent-up energy of our windbound captivity.

Wave-worn points of rock and quiet beaches slip past; a bull moose looks up from where it feeds at the mouth of a shallow stream. A loon calls in the distance.

By the time we decide to look for a campsite, the sky is orange with sunset and we've covered a dozen miles. A small, domed bedrock island looks worth investigating, so we angle in. A deep cleft in the rock makes a perfect one-canoe garage. At the top of the island, in a fringe of stubby spruce, we discover a flat opening layered with sphagnum moss just the right size for the tent. There are blueberries weighing down the bushes.

The George River, Quebec (Photo: ©Alan Kesselheim)

We've been out almost a week, so the drill of unpacking, securing the boat for the night, setting up the tent, and arranging our bags and pads inside is accomplished with quick efficiency. We opt for an easy dinner of macaroni and cheese, cooked on top of the stove, followed by a bowl full of ripe island blueberries.

The western sky is purple with the last of the northern sunset by the time we've cleaned up dishes, covered the packs with a tarp, and put our clothes bags in the tent. We heat water for tea and take the steaming mugs to an opening in the trees that overlooks the lake. It is utterly quiet. The lake is so still it doesn't even lap against shore.

Then a pair of loons swim into view around the tip of the island, sharp silhouettes mirrored in the water. Three more appear, then another pair. Finally, more than twenty loons parade in front of us, as if they are the neighborhood welcome committee come to pay a visit. The sleek birds swim slowly past without a sound and disappear again behind the curve of the island.

The first stars show in the darkening sky. We find the constellation Scorpio in the west, then the Dippers and the North Star, Polaris. Just before we head for the tent, there is an outburst from the loons, a wild chorus of wailing that fills the night. Then silence again.

Much later, when I wake in the muffled darkness, the air still seems to echo with loon song.

PRETRIP PLANNING

Much of the quality of your camping experience is predestined by the thoroughness you devote to preparing for a trip before you ever leave your driveway. Planning a careful itinerary, bringing appropriate gear, organizing a nutritious menu, and forming a cohesive group of travel partners reaps benefits in campsite after campsite once you are in the field. The main planning issues are common to all journeys, and several impact the complexion of your time in camp in important ways.

Itinerary

A medley of factors contribute to the itinerary. How much time do you have? How much money is in the budget? What are your paddling skills? Do you plan on side excursions? Is your craft a sleek downriver canoe or an 18-foot paddle raft? Is your destination full of lakes and portages, or characterized by steady river current with few obstacles? Addressing both the questions of logistics (time available, mileage to cover) and personal style (side trips, desired pace) will help you come up with a realistic plan.

Figuring miles per day. On a river with steady current and minor obstacles, a canoeist or kayaker might make 30 miles in a reasonable day. At the same time, a route marked with many lakes and long portages could slow you down to 10 miles a day or less. A heavily loaded raft on slow water going against a head wind has trouble getting around the bend, much less making miles, while a light, fast canoe with two strong paddlers can put miles behind it by the dozen. Beyond that, wind and weather delays, side explorations, and rest days erode the travel pace further.

As a rule of thumb for planning, 15 miles per day is a good starting point. On a trip with varied water and for a range of watercraft, 15 miles is a pretty reasonable daily goal.

Carefully measure the overall distance on the topographic map or river guide. (River guides may already be marked mile by mile.) On topographic maps, lay a piece of flexible string along your route and measure it against the scale on the bottom. You can also buy a map wheel if you want to be very precise. Don't rely on road miles or on measurements taken from general maps, because the figures are prone to significant error. Divide the total distance by the number of travel days to calculate your daily average: for example, 120 miles divided by 8 days equals 15 miles per day.

You may want to itemize your mileage between flat water and moving water to get a more accurate handle on a realistic pace. If 80 percent of your time will be on fast-moving rivers, you might bump the mileage estimate up to as much as 20 miles per day. If your route involves lake crossings and portages, and you like bird-watching side trips, consider 10 or 12 miles per day. If anything, err on the conservative side. There is nothing worse than struggling to meet an unrealistic but inflexible deadline and missing out on the rewards of wilderness immersion.

General map study. At the same time you figure your daily mileage average, scrutinize the maps closely—kind of a living room scouting trip. Study the route for portages, rapids, large lake crossings, the topography along coastlines, big chunks of swampy land, and so on. You can often isolate a trip's obvious challenges and then plan your campsites accordingly. Camp at the beginning of a series of portages, for instance, so you don't get stuck halfway across. Allow plenty of time to negotiate tricky white water. Avoid having to stop in swampy lowlands where sites may be limited and insects fierce.

Look for likely places to explore—ridges, nearby peaks, side canyons—and tentatively set up your itinerary with the flexibility to stop there. If a lakeshore has miles of exposed shoreline along one coast but is full of bays and islands along the other, you may want to plan your route to take advantage of the protection and camping variety offered by the more convoluted shore.

In general, better campsites are located at the tips of peninsulas, on minor ridges, on islands, and at spots either just upstream or downstream of rapids. Once you compute your mileage average, look over the maps to see the kinds of landforms available at roughly that interval, and highlight the places where campsites may be most dubious.

Camping restrictions. Heavily used areas like the Boundary Waters in Minnesota or the Grand Canyon in Arizona are controlled by permits and designated campsites, while less-used destinations are accessible to less-restricted camping. Be sure you understand any camping limitations before you head off. (Some areas have stream-access laws that allow camping on islands and below high-water marks, while others don't even permit boaters to stop along sections of private land.)

Carrying capacity. Camping by canoe, kayak, or raft is forgiving in that the boat shoulders the gear load and has space to grant you a measure of luxury along with the ability to stay out longer than backpackers, skiers, or bikers. Trips of a month or more without resupply are certainly possible, and a journey of two weeks or more is quite a reasonable goal.

Rafts are the real cargo mules of water travel. You can pile them high with folding tables, Dutch ovens, camp chairs, ice chests, and drinking water by the gallon. Kayaks are the least roomy craft and require the most attention to weight and bulk. Most tripping canoes are rated to carry a maximum load of between 800 and 1,200 pounds (including people), but you'd be hard pressed to fit that much in unless your cargo runs to sacks of concrete. Keep in mind, however, that the heavier your load, the more unwieldy the boat will be on the water and the more time you'll spend corralling gear. Just because you have the room doesn't mean you have to fill it up!

Resupplies. On long journeys, food, fuel, film, and even some gear may need to be replenished along the way. These resupply stops are disruptive to a trip's rhythm; they are often expensive and logistically cumbersome. If you can get away without them, do so. If you can't avoid a resupply and there are towns en route, you can indulge in a little shopping excursion. (Beware, however, of towns that on the map look like they are located right on the water but may, in fact, involve a serious hike to reach them—and the nearest store.) Better yet, mail yourself packages to that town care of General Delivery. (Contact the post office in question to make sure it'll hold your boxes.) Sending your own care package ahead of time is more dependable than relying on local stores to have what you need at affordable prices. In less populated regions, you may have to set your own supply caches at access points, or arrange to be met by charter plane or vehicle. Make sure you really nail down the details if your trip is contingent on such a plan.

▲ ▲ ▲

Boating Pretrip Checklist

Early On (as much as a year ahead)

- Explore the time available and set general dates.
- Sift through destination and route choices.
- Decide the ballpark budget.
- Settle on the ideal group size and start making contacts.
- Think through the overall trip goals.

Middle Range (three to six months ahead)

- Finalize trip logistics (route, dates, resupplies, shuttles).
- Nail down trip commitment and set the group membership and financial contribution.
- Delegate responsibilities (food planning, gear, itinerary, shuttle, et cetera).
- Focus the search for route information.
- Start organizing any problematic travel logistics.
- Choose menu strategy (dried, store-bought, strong personal preferences).
- Discuss and refine trip goals.

Down to the Wire (final months/weeks)

- Purchase, prep, and pack food.
- Organize, customize, and purchase gear.
- Hold group meetings or phone/fax communication to nail down logistics.
- Do final route research and map study; set itinerary.
- Discuss trip goals and personal ambitions.
- Do final packing (ideally as a group, so everyone is involved).

Rafts can carry amenities like ice chests full of fresh food and Dutch ovens and charcoal for baking. (Photo: ©Alan Kesselheim)

Group Selection Process

In the case of solo travel or trips with your spouse and/or family, your group is predestined; but if you're forming a loosely defined group, start early on. Some trip societies have a unifying theme—old college friends, women's trips, family reunions—in which case the pool of partners is largely set. More often, we invite a collection of friends and hope for a congenial gathering of companions.

Give people plenty of notice, so that they can mull the trip over and work out logistics. Invite a few extra people on the expectation that not everyone will be able to go, but don't overdo it. It can really harm a friendship if you have to turn someone down because the group size has gotten out of hand. From the start, be as clear as you can about the trip, what skills and experience are necessary, the length and difficulty of the route, and what your expectations are.

Food Organization

Water travel often allows the luxury of bringing fresh food and even refrigerated food in coolers, in the case of canoes and rafts (as long as the portages are few and short!). At least for the first few days (before the ice melts or food spoils), you can enjoy fresh meals unheard of on most wilderness trips. Even when space is precious, it is usually possible to squeeze in a few fresh onions, some resilient fruits and vegetables, or a little fresh meat.

For long trips, the food supplies can become pretty daunting and unruly. If you're off for more than two weeks, the amount of food necessary is downright shocking. Without a systematic plan of organization, it will seem that half your time in camp is spent rummaging through packs in search of spices, the evening meal, or that elusive dessert.

Truly systematic paddlers prepackage their food into daily numbered sacks. On Day 7, they know just which bag to grab, and their food search is over. If you rebel against such meticulous preparation (or don't have the time . . . or don't want to be constrained to a menu that may not jibe with conditions in the field), you can at least strive for some middle ground.

Separate the food by breakfast, lunch, dinner, and pantry (drinks, spices, condiments, treats) categories. Bag up one-meal or one-serving amounts (in waterproof bags), and then pack them into color-coded stuff sacks: blue for breakfast, for example, red for lunch. Or mark them with strips of colored tape or pieces of colored yarn.

Include a small dry bag or hip sack to carry the day's lunch. Pack it each morning before leaving camp and load it in an accessible spot, so you won't have to dig through mounds of gear at lunch. Tight-sealing plastic boxes (in various sizes) are the modern equivalent of traditional wannigans (wood kitchen boxes), and are good for protecting the vulnerable pots, stoves, and other kitchen gear on canoe or raft trips with few portages.

▲ ▲ ▲

Special Kitchen Gear for Boating

Water containers. Even if you don't need to carry potable water, a two-and-a-half-gallon collapsible water jug minimizes trips to the water source. The liner bladders from boxed wine containers work well as durable water bags with good pour spouts.

Dutch ovens. When cooking on fires, cast-aluminum, cast-iron, or other types of Dutch oven open up the world of baked goods, roast meats, pizzas, and the like. It can also double as the large cook pot.

Reflector ovens. Traditional boating camps that use fires routinely carry folding reflector ovens to cook biscuits and other baked delights.

Pressure cookers. Small, lightweight pressure cookers reduce cooking times and allow you to include bulk staples such as brown rice and beans.

Grills. When you're relying on fires, a cook grill with adjustable legs is a great asset. Make sure it comes with a stuff sack, so you can keep the rest of your gear free of fire soot.

Stoves. Two- and three-burner stoves, or models built into folding tables, expand the culinary horizons.

Fire pans. Garbage can lids or 2-foot-by-2-foot squares of tin with the edges turned up (and smoothed) work well to contain the cook fire or campfire and to negate the legacy of fire scars for future campers.

Boating Tents and Shelters

Boaters, with the exception of those using low-volume kayaks, have the opportunity to camp in relatively large and heavy tents. These have the benefits of greater head room, space for extra clothes bags, big windows, and more floor space. Roomy vestibules allow for extra storage or for cooking in stormy weather. The only caveat is that some large tents are tall and quite susceptible to strong winds. Make sure you can stake the tent securely and that the design isn't overly blocky.

Boaters have the luxury of taking large tents. (Photo: ©Alan Kesselheim)

In addition to large tents, take a roomy tarp (10 feet by 12 feet is adequate for four or five people) for shade or rain shelter, or to cook under. A coated nylon tarp with plenty of cord tied to the grommet holes is very handy.

Clothing

For an itemized clothing list, consult the Equipment Checklist in this chapter. Also see the Clothing section of Pretrip Planning in chapter 1 for a thorough discussion of camp clothing. Clothes for paddling are distinguished by their quick-drying characteristics. Paddlers also need footwear that can be wet much of the time. As with the rest of the paddler's outfit, it is often possible to get away with heavier and bulkier clothing (foul-weather gear, for instance) than with other outdoor pursuits.

Waterproofing Gear

Dry bags (which range in size from ditty sacks to massive packs with shoulder straps) are the most efficient and failproof waterproofing strategy. However, outfitting yourself with an entire array of dry bags is an expensive proposition. It makes sense to have several dry bags for the clothes you want handy for the day, your journal and camera, and so on, but clothes and bulky gear can go into canvas packs (known as Duluth packs) or backpacks lined with heavy-mil plastic bags. (Grocery-store garbage bags are not adequate. Try discount stores or outdoor equipment outlets for the heavy-duty varieties, and take along spares.)

Portable Toilets

Because riparian corridors and coastlines are so vulnerable to water pollution problems, and because boating campsites are often used repeatedly, portable toilets are sometimes required of boating parties (even if not required, they may be environmentally sensible).

Homemade Portable Toilet

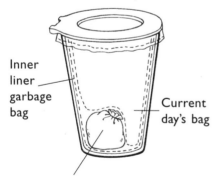

Five-gallon bucket with screw-on or snap-on lid

Inner liner garbage bag

Current day's bag

One day's bag full of waste, sprinkled with powdered bleach and closed up

Recreational vehicle (RV) suppliers, powerboat dealers, and outdoor retailers that carry rafting supplies are the best places to shop for portable toilets. You can either spend the money for a self-contained, ready-to-use model, or create a homemade version. On some heavily used rivers, commercial portable toilets that can be dumped at an RV dump station are required. The simplest homemade portable toilets utilize a five-gallon plastic bucket with a snap-on or screw-on lid, or a large army-surplus ammo can with a reliable seal. Also bring a supply of heavy-mil plastic bags that fit the container. Bring some bleach powder to reduce odor. If you have room and want the extra comfort, carry along a toilet seat to place on top of the bucket.

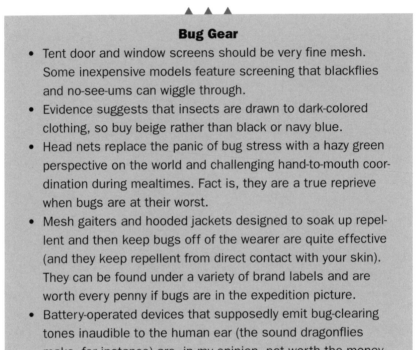

▲ ▲ ▲

Bug Gear

- Tent door and window screens should be very fine mesh. Some inexpensive models feature screening that blackflies and no-see-ums can wiggle through.
- Evidence suggests that insects are drawn to dark-colored clothing, so buy beige rather than black or navy blue.
- Head nets replace the panic of bug stress with a hazy green perspective on the world and challenging hand-to-mouth coordination during mealtimes. Fact is, they are a true reprieve when bugs are at their worst.
- Mesh gaiters and hooded jackets designed to soak up repellent and then keep bugs off of the wearer are quite effective (and they keep repellent from direct contact with your skin). They can be found under a variety of brand labels and are worth every penny if bugs are in the expedition picture.
- Battery-operated devices that supposedly emit bug-clearing tones inaudible to the human ear (the sound dragonflies make, for instance) are, in my opinion, not worth the money.

Insect Repellents

Because water travel means you may be in prime bug habitat, think about insect avoidance. There are no panaceas for buggy camps, but a few aids will help in bug zones. Remember that trips taken in the fall tend to bypass the height of bug season (the trade-off is iffy weather prospects).

The bulk of mainstream insect dope utilizes the active ingredient DEET (N, N-diethyl-m-toluamide) to deter bugs. Some brands tout 100 percent DEET content, but 30 percent DEET concentration in repellents is quite sufficient. There is no arguing that DEET is effective; unfortunately, DEET is also toxic. Although research hasn't documented clear health hazards from normal use of DEET repellents, it should be kept out of eyes, the mouth, and open cuts. DEET also corrodes plastics (camera bodies, paddle shafts, et cetera). If you opt to use DEET because of its effectiveness, use it sparingly (a drop on the end of your nose rather than smearing it on, or a light application here and there on clothing cuffs rather than directly on your skin). Try to avoid leaving DEET on your palms and fingers.

An array of "friendlier" repellents have been developed in response to the problems with DEET. Most of these have a strong dose of citronella, mixed with alcohol, other oils, and fragrances. My experience has been that they aren't as foolproof as DEET, but I can live with a slightly elevated level of bug stress in trade for a more benign product.

A variety of dietary bug-away cures also have proponents. For instance, high doses of B vitamins or eating quantities of garlic before a trip are supposed to ward off the insect world, but I can't say that I've found any of these to be particularly effective.

Avon's "Skin So Soft" lotion is purported to have bug-chasing properties, and certainly has the advantage of a more pleasant odor (not to mention moisturizing qualities) over most repellents. I've found it to be only somewhat effective.

▲ ▲ ▲

Equipment Checklist for Boating

This is a very complete and comprehensive list. Adapt it to fit the conditions of your journey and your craft. For instance, an August weekend outing in Arizona probably doesn't require head nets or long underwear.

Kitchen Gear
- matches (in several waterproof containers)
- hatchet and/or small saw (if using fires)
- cook grill with adjustable legs (for fires)
- stove(s)
- gas or fuel bottles
- large water containers (a collapsible two-and-a-half-gallon container is handy even on trips where you don't have to carry fresh water)

- large pot or cast aluminum Dutch oven or pressure cooker (depending on conditions)
- medium pot
- fry pan or small griddle
- small, thin plastic cutting board (optional)
- pot lifters
- scrubby and biodegradable soap
- large spoon
- small metal spatula
- large knife or fillet knife (optional)
- coffee filter (optional)
- water filter/pump (if necessary)
- fire pan (when appropriate)
- garbage bags

Group Equipment

- tent(s) with rain fly
- ground cloth (optional)
- cooking tarp (10-foot-by-12-foot for a group of four or five)
- large-capacity packs and/or boxes (dry bags, soft packs, frame packs, tight-sealing plastic boxes)
- boat(s) (canoe, kayak, raft, or combination)
- paddles or oars (with spare)
- bow and stern lines (canoes and rafts)
- rowing frame and/or flooring (rafts)
- tie-down cord or straps (canoes and rafts)
- bailers and/or pumps (for water that collects in boats)
- sponge (kayaks and rafts)
- paddle floats (kayaks)
- pump (to inflate rafts)
- toilet paper (optional)
- portable toilet (mostly for rafting trips)
- solar shower (optional)
- folding or roll-up camp table (optional)
- small trowel (for digging cat holes and moving coals if cooking on open fires)
- maps (one set per boat ideally)

- compass (kayakers sometimes mount them on the deck)
- map wheel (optional)

Personal Clothing
- camp shoes (light hikers, tennis shoes, moccasins)
- water shoes (sandals, slip-ons, shoes that dry quickly)
- neoprene boots/socks (only for really cold water or extended wading)
- three to four pairs of socks (several thicknesses)
- quick-drying pants or shorts
- long pants (canvas, light wool, khaki)
- long underwear tops and bottoms (not cotton!)
- wind pants and jacket (good for buggy or blustery days, and quick drying)
- rain suit
- underwear
- T-shirts (two or three depending on trip length)
- long-sleeve shirt
- vest or heavy shirt or light jacket
- bandanna
- visor or brim hat
- light gloves or mittens
- wool hat
- bug jacket and/or headnet (in buggy country)

Personal Gear
- toilet kit (with any personal medications)
- assorted waterproof bags (dry bags, heavy-mil plastic, resealable) for maps, books, clothing, et cetera
- sleeping pad
- sleeping bag
- sleeping bag liner (optional)
- insect repellent
- eating utensils (cup, bowl, and spoon generally suffice for most occasions)
- waterproof matchsafe
- pocket knife (I tie mine with a cord to my belt)
- life vest

- folding camp chair (optional, but very nice!)
- sunglasses
- personal water bottle
- waterproof bag or box for camera, binoculars, maps, journal, et cetera
- reading book or journal plus pencil or pen (optional)
- fishing tackle (optional)
- camera plus lens and film (optional)
- binoculars (optional)
- flashlight (and candles, optional)
- day pack or hip sack (for excursions or as an accessible pack in the boat)
- playing cards or other compact games (optional)

Safety and Repair Gear

- throw rope and three or four carabiners
- bear protection (pepper spray canisters)
- Emergency Location Transmitter (for really remote or extended wilderness immersion)
- sewing kit (include zipper sliders, some velcro, et cetera)
- boat patch/repair kit
- general repair kit (duct tape, small pliers and screwdriver, stove wrench, spare gaskets, seam-seal, spare tent stakes, et cetera)
- complete first-aid kit with prescription medications if needed

Boat Camping Is Great for Families

Outdoor travel by boat is excellent family recreation for one simple reason: The boat carries both people and gear. Essentially every other outdoor activity (aside from horse packing, perhaps) requires parents to carry, tow, or pull youngsters along, or to put up with the complaints of older children who don't rise above the discomfort of physical exertion to revel in the joys of outdoor living.

Boats, particularly canoes or rafts, are truly the recreational vehicles of the self-powered crowd. Not only do they carry the human cargo, but their spaciousness allows the possibility of everything from diaper pails to volleyball nets.

Because little ones are often hypersensitive to bug bites, time your trip with an eye to missing high bug season. Be ready to retire to the tent early if bugs are fierce, and bring long pants and a long-sleeved shirt for each child to protect vulnerable skin.

That same clothing will shield tender skin from intense sun. Make sure infants wear sun hats with adequate visors and flaps in back to protect their necks. Lather on the sunscreen over exposed areas.

Rain and cold are particularly tough on kids. In most cases they won't be working as hard (which generates heat) as the adults. Even if all else is equal, children have to work harder to generate body heat than their parents do. Allow yourself plenty of extra time so you can wait out inclement weather. Outfit children with adequate rain gear (tops and bottoms, or good ponchos) and plenty of changes of warm clothes. Hypothermia is not a family experience that builds character or lends itself to fond memories!

Three kids in a tub! Boating is a great family activity because the craft can carry young kids and all their accoutrements. (Photo: ©Marypat Zitzer)

Here are some tips for family-style boating.

1. Travel water on which you feel absolutely confident. This is no time to push your skill envelope.
2. Take a boat you are comfortable with and skilled at maneuvering. If you are at home in a canoe, fine. If not, try a raft.
3. Pad your itinerary to allow for weather delays, explorations, and short days.
4. Pick a route with reasonable accessibility to towns or roads, in the event of emergencies.
5. Invite friends and family. Other children, extra adults, or grandparents are great assets.
6. Kids will find lots to occupy themselves with, but bring some distractions along too. Older kids can lose themselves in books and enjoy tossing a ball or other camp activities. Toddlers are content with a bucket, a small shovel, and a few toys.
7. Food diversions are essential. Dried fruit, licorice sticks, some candy, powdered drink mixes, and hot cocoa quiet kids in times of stress.

There are additional considerations when you have infants and toddlers in a boating camp.

1. Bring a kid-carrier backpack to free you for side excursions, and to keep your hands free for chores.
2. A low-tech, hand-crank food mill renders whatever the adults are eating into baby gruel.
3. Chewy dried fruit (especially bananas sliced the long way before drying) are great teething foods.
4. Toddlers have an endless capacity for throwing rocks in the water. A bucketful can be a great distraction. Make sure the rocks aren't small enough to present a choking hazard should they end up in a toddler's mouth.
5. Infant and toddler life vests should fit snugly, have leg loops to prevent them from slipping over the head, and be very buoyant at the top and behind the head so the youngster will bob upright, face out of the water.
6. Youngsters should wear life vests whenever they're near the water, even onshore.

A kid pack is useful for day hikes and frees your hands for camp chores. (Photo: ©Marypat Zitzer)

SETTING UP CAMP

Finally, you are on the water. All the preparation has focused down to this spot on the map, this group of people, this collection of gear and food and boats. You are nomads, water travelers, and a significant quota of group energy will be devoted to the task of finding a site and settling in at each day's home.

When to Stop

Because you figured out the mileage you need to cover, you'll have a vague daily goal. Even before you leave camp in the morning, you can forecast generally where you'd like to stop, and you may even study the map to check for likely possibilities.

Don't let the daily average trap you into an inflexible regimen, however. Some days bring tail winds and steady current, others head winds and a handful of portages. There will be days when group energy is hitting on all cylinders, others when it seems as if the engine is running on maple syrup.

Assess the weather constantly as you travel. Thunderheads tend to build up during the day and strike at late afternoon or evening, by which time you'd like to be protected and secure. Afternoon winds are the bane of trips on large lakes. Better to rise before dawn in order to make miles and camp early than to push on in dangerous surf. Cold, wet weather can lead to hypothermia. Stop before people are shivering and soaked, even if it means falling behind your anticipated schedule.

Take stock of the group energy toward the end of the day. Pushing for one more mile, one last rapid, or a final portage after a long day on the water is asking for trouble. Base decisions on the most fatigued or least skilled paddlers. Better an early camp than a capsize in white water or a twisted ankle on a portage trail.

Stop with plenty of daylight left to set up camp and comfortably prepare the evening meal. Once you get practiced at the drill, you can have the tents up and dinner served in an hour or less. In the first days, however, allow 2 or 3 hours to get the bugs worked out.

Choosing a Boating Campsite

We all have a collage of mental images for great campsites—pristine desert beaches, an open jack pine forest, polished bedrock, a northern island weighed down with ripe blueberries. These are what we look for as the day wears on and the pressure to find a nice camp mounts.

Stop and scout prospective camps. Sometimes what looks perfect from the water is actually full of poison ivy and lumpy tent sites. Conversely, an unassuming, dense shoreline may obscure a beautiful and protected forest glade. When scouting, look for the following:

- a good landing with plenty of room to tie the boats up or pull them onto shore
- protected water for launching (river eddy, bay, calm water behind a point)
- plenty of room for tents without having to crowd each other, as well as for the kitchen site and portable toilet location (if needed)
- shelter from wind and weather (tree cover, overhang, et cetera)
- safety from environmental danger (not at the narrow mouth of a desert side canyon during flash flood season, for example, or at the base of a steep, rain-saturated mud bank, or beneath an isolated towering tree with a lightning storm brewing)

- an elevated, breezy spot for relief from insects
- access to enticing excursions—side canyons, ridges, low peaks, fun scrambling rocks

Finally, beware the dangerous game of "campsite roulette," wherein you pass up an idyllic spot because it's a tad early in the day, then another pretty camp because you want to get past the next rapid, yet another because you're sure there will be more around the bend. Suddenly it's twilight and the nice campsites have evaporated, leaving you to set up in the middle of marshy lowlands.

Bugs. For all the benefits accrued by water travel, the one significant downside is that water is also the preferred habitat for many insect species whose mission on earth seems focused on making life miserable for paddlers. When you choose a campsite in bug season, avoid low, swampy areas with lots of standing water. Even a slight elevation or ridge is often enough to afford a bug-clearing breeze. Open areas (beaches or clearings) tend to be less bug infested than dense, shady spots. Mosquitoes, blackflies, no-see-ums, deer flies—they all have their habitats, niches, and seasons. It's nearly impossible to avoid all bug conditions.

Unpacking and Stowing the Boats

As soon as you land, everyone should pitch in to unload. Kayakers are each responsible for their own gear once their boats are pulled up onshore. Raft and canoe parties should unload with the boats still in the water to avoid scraping and damaging the hulls (exceptions to this include landings with crashing surf or powerful river current).

Usually, one person stays aboard to untie gear while others hold (or secure) the boat and take equipment to the campsite. If camp is some distance away or conditions at the landing are rough, simply pile gear onshore until the boats are empty.

Unless you are concerned about theft or dangerous winds, boating gear can be secured at the launch site. Paddles, bailers, pumps, life vests, tie-down straps, and the like should be cleaned up and stowed inside or underneath the boats, protected from sudden winds or bumping waves. All the other packs and parcels go up to a central gear location (often near the camp kitchen).

Remember that your boats are your life-support craft and, often, your only way out of the backcountry. Secure them for the night with

To save effort, scout your campsite first, then unload gear and take it directly to the area—camp kitchen or tent site—where it belongs. (Photo: ©Marypat Zitzer)

that thought in mind. Even if conditions are balmy, ask yourself what would happen if a sudden squall with strong winds whipped up, if waves started pounding in, or if the river level rose a foot. Then put the boats out of harm's way. Be sure the boats are well clear of the reach of tides, waves, or rising water, and settled where they aren't exposed to direct wind.

Kayaks and canoes should come well up onshore. Any excess water inside should be bailed or sponged out. Mud, sand, and dirt may periodically need to be cleaned off. Canoes should be turned over each night, with loose gear placed underneath. My practice is to always tie my canoe to a rock or tree. More than once I've seen winds pick up and fling a canoe down the shore.

Rafts should be left in the water (sometimes they can be pulled partly onto a smooth shore). After cleaning them out for the day, tether them securely to a tree, stout stake, or heavy rock. Take a minute to observe how they ride in the water. Make sure they aren't chafing against sharp rocks or sticks, resting on anything abrasive, or rubbing against each other dangerously. Even after you've been in camp a while, it's good practice to check the rafts periodically. It isn't uncommon to have to retie them several times.

Arrival in Camp

Get in the habit of assuming the worst and pack accordingly. In other words, assume that when you stop for the day, it will be twilight, windy, and raining, and the insect hordes will be thick. Wind and rain often come as a combination package, and even when they don't, the coping strategies are similar. To begin with, strong winds or a storm may force you to stop early and make do with a less-than-ideal campsite.

In these circumstances your goal is to be fast, efficient, and safe. A well-organized setup drill is crucial to staying safe and comfortable. The first step in responding to storm and wind is to protect yourself with adequate rain or wind gear, which should always be accessible. The rain fly should be at the top of the load. If it's raining when you stop, your first task is to pitch the tarp and get gear and people underneath. With that shelter in place, you can tackle the other chores.

Tents, a stove, and some quick energy food (instant soup, hot cocoa, granola bars) should also be handy. One person can boil water for hot drinks while the tents are being set up. Other gear that needs to be handy includes insect repellent, rain gear, and warm jackets. Once the basic shelters are up, people have changed into dry, warm clothes, and a round of hot drinks has gone down, you can deal with sleeping bags, dinner, and the rest of camp details at a more sedate pace. Even under benign conditions, setting up efficiently rewards you with extra free time to relax and explore.

Not everyone needs to be involved in every chore. One person can set up the camp kitchen, another the portable toilet, one or two more the tent(s); yet another can prepare the evening meal. Rotate the chores so that everyone gets relief from repeated tasks. If you have enough people (or a really efficient team), you may even be able to award one or two group members a day off from camp drudgery from time to time.

When you stow canoes for the night, secure them to each other and to a tree, rock, or some other anchor so they won't blow away if the wind comes up. (Photo: ©Marypat Zitzer)

Dressing for Camp Comfort

Strip off those wet, clammy river shoes, set them where they'll dry out (or out of the rain), and pull on dry camp shoes or moccasins. At the top of my priority list, almost without exception, is a set of dry, warm shoes and socks. While you're at it, adjust the rest of your clothing to fit camp life: a pair of long pants, a long-sleeved shirt, a vest. A dry change of clothes is an affirmation of the transition from boat to shore life, and from day to evening.

If you've arrived in stormy weather, assess your own (and your companions') condition. Adjust clothing layers so that you are warm and dry, even if it means delaying other camp chores. Remember, hypothermia often strikes in weather that doesn't seem particularly extreme, and can result when people ignore their deteriorating level of comfort.

Rehydrate

That afternoon gap between paddling and dinner often begs for a round of drinks and a bite to eat. Hot cocoa or instant soup fills the bill on cold days, or a cold powdered drink mix on a hot afternoon. At the same time, pass around a bag of trail mix or dried fruit. The snack break is a good point to regroup, discuss the day's events, and make sure all camp chores will be taken care of.

If you're setting up camp in rainy or windy weather, once camp is set, boil water for hot drinks, either under the cook tarp or in a tent vestibule. With the shelters in place and everyone reasonably warm and dry, you can then make the rounds to be sure all the gear is accounted for and protected, and that the boats are adequately stowed.

Pitching Tents in Boating Campsites

On rivers and coastlines good tent sites may be strictly confined to a small beach, a pebbly flat, or a limited opening in thick brush. It is not always feasible to camp the standard 200 feet from the nearest water, but be as sensitive as you can be, both to the proximity to water and to your neighbor's need for privacy (especially if you are a renowned snorer).

Sand is a very common element in boating camps, and it is both a joy and a curse. Sand makes comfy and groomable sleeping surfaces, and is easy to maintain in terms of leaving no trace. On the other hand, sand is a poor staking medium and has a way of worming its way into everything. Finally, sand beaches tend to be exposed to wind and weather.

If a storm or high winds look imminent, seek out a more protected tent site in the forest or brush, even if it's tougher to work with initially. Pitch camp, as much as possible, on firm ground (not sand) and under the protection of trees, brush, or on the least exposed topography. Wind-blown and/or wet sand is a boater's nemesis. If a storm strikes after you've already set up in sand and a more protected patch of solid ground is nearby, it is usually worth the trouble of relocating. If you opt for sand, weigh down the tent guy lines with rocks, tie them to driftwood logs, or use very long tent stakes to nail down your shelter.

In a storm, tents should sit backside to the wind and rain and be guyed to solid stakes, rocks, or brush. In a real gale it may take all of you to wrestle the tarp and tents one at a time. Get the sleeping bags, clothes bags, and other gear that must stay dry into the tents, underneath canoes, or under the tarp. (Tent vestibules are handy for this.)

Be ruthless in your quest to keep the tent a sand-free zone! Brush off before you enter, remove your shoes outside, and dust off every item before it goes in. Besides the discomfort of sand in your sleeping bag, in your clothes, and in your journal, it is one of the biggest culprits in tent zipper failure. It only takes one trip in bug country with a tent door that won't close to cure your love of sandy beaches!

Stowing Sleeping Gear
Unroll and/or inflate the sleeping pads and place them in the sleeping spots (if you have plenty of floor space, avoid direct contact with the tent walls). Lie down to check whether there is any noticeable slope, either head to toe or side to side. If so, orient your head uphill and manicure the surface or shift the pads to minimize side slope. Lay out the bags, along with liners if you have them. (Liners can be as simple as a rectangular envelope sewn from a cotton or flannel sheet. They add a layer of insulation, keep the bags clean, and, in hot, muggy weather, you can sleep in the liner alone.)

Siting a Portable Toilet
As much as possible, set the portable toilet 200 feet from the main camp and camp kitchen and seclude it behind some vegetation or topographic cover. Also keep it 200 feet from water sources.

THE CAMP KITCHEN
Much attention gets lavished on tent sites with award-winning views, but the fact is that most of your tent time is spent with the door closed and your eyes shut. The camp kitchen and eating area is actually the focus of waking hours in camp, and the place from which we're most likely to enjoy (or be inflicted with) the qualities of our temporary home. Apply the same criteria to your camp kitchen that you do to tent locations: good view, protection from elements, bug-clearing breeze, 200 feet from water if possible, and so on.

In addition, remember that the camp kitchen will be the campsite hub. As such, it should be central and accessible. However, choose a cook site that is off the main camp thoroughfares and protected from boisterous activities (tossing games, water fights, kids playing, et cetera). You'll also want adequate space for everyone to sit and relax during meals, along with a comfortable prep area for the cook(s) to work in.

Site the kitchen along a corridor connecting it to the boat launch, so the carry isn't overly cumbersome. Try to be at least 200 feet from shore

Canoes can be set up to provide a convenient work surface as well as a windbreak on breezy days. (Photo: ©Dorcas Miller)

to minimize the chance of contamination from soap, gray water, or food waste. If possible, the cooking and eating area should be 100 feet from the nearest tent, because nocturnal critters are drawn to stray food scraps or odors.

The Cook Tarp

One of the first things I look for is a spot to string the cook tarp (a 10-foot-by-12-foot tarp is adequate for four or five people). In weather that requires using the heat source under a tarp for shelter, consider the fire or stove site when you choose where to pitch the tarp.

There are an endless number of tarp structures, but two trees or branches spaced roughly 15 feet apart serve nicely. The front edge of the tarp can be aligned between those two tie points and fastened about 8 feet up. Slope the tarp down to the back edge and tie it off at 4 feet from the ground to lower branches, sticks, or paddles. This simple shelter protects you from direct sun or rain; it allows the cook(s) to stand and work comfortably at the high end, and packs and gear can be stowed dry at the low end. (Orient the open end away from the prevailing winds!) In

Tarps can be draped over a line, propped up in the center with a well-padded paddle or stick, set up with the full surface facing the wind, or set up in other configurations. (Photos: ©Marypat Zitzer)

stormy conditions, rig the high end of the cook tarp to face away from the wind and rain, and secure good anchors on the windward side.

To create additional head room or space for more people, prop a kayak paddle, oar, or long stick under the center of the tarp to elevate the ceiling (pad the end that rests against the tarp with a bandanna). Or, if you have four good tie points and a long, stout center pole, tie off the four corners as high as you can reach and prop the pole securely under the center.

Organizing the Camp Kitchen

Think of your camp kitchen much as you do your kitchen at home. You'll need the same basic elements: a cooking surface, a prep surface, and a serving/organizing space. The equipment pack and food bags serve as your cupboards.

Collect all the food and cooking supplies and set them up at the rear of the camp kitchen. Set the stove (or site the fire) on level ground clear of flammable brush. A slight elevation makes for more convenient stove cooking (the top of a large, flat boulder, for instance), but don't sacrifice stove stability for height. An elevated platform also helps reduce the chance of someone tripping over the stove, and minimizes sand or dirt getting in the cook pot (or in the working parts of the stove).

A roll-up or folding table is ideal for both a prep surface and an organizing space. Tables are, however, a luxury in the backcountry. Coolers (or tight-sealing plastic boxes available from paddling retailers) are a good substitute surface for cutting up and organizing food. Barring tables and coolers/boxes, a small, thin, hard plastic cutting board (roughly 6 inches by 12 inches by ¼ inch) is a very handy and compact work surface. Beyond that, make do with what's at hand to create the kitchen furniture—a flat rock for a small table, a stump for a chair, a downed log for an organizing platform.

If you're the day's chef, make yourself comfortable. I like to sit on an ammo can or rock with the necessary food and utensils within reach. Some cooks prefer to stand and move around as they create, while others fancy a folding chair or small pad set on the ground.

The biggest challenge in boat camp kitchens is to manage the ubiquitous clouds of sand. If possible, cook off the ground to avoid chance spills or kicked-up grit. Try to find a cook spot on firm soil, a flat rock, or

Look around for a convenient location to use as your camp kitchen.
(Photo: ©Marypat Zitzer)

another stable platform away from sand. Keep your utensils and dishes on a table, rock, or stuff sack. Make a habit of always brushing off the bottoms of cups or bowls before you dip them into the pot.

Cooking with Fires

More and more, the rule of thumb in the backcountry is to go fireless. Boating trips are, arguably, the most prevalent exception to that rule, for several reasons.

To begin with, boaters often have the space available to bring along a fire pan to protect the ground from scarring. Beyond that, rafters and canoeists may be able to bring their own supply of charcoal briquettes and collect driftwood during the day. Rivers, lakeshores, and coastlines are often rich with driftwood.

Fires can either be built in fire pans or on mineral soil (sand and gravel free of vegetation) below the high-water mark. A cook fire grants you a large cook area, the ability to bake with coals, and the chance to reduce the amount of bulky and expensive stove fuel you have to cart along. The use of a cook fire, however, has a significant impact on the siting of the kitchen (below high-water mark, for example, and well clear of flammable vegetation).

At the same time, the environmental caveats that have made fires taboo throughout much of North American wilderness still apply. Campfires are only appropriate in sites with plenty of down and dead wood (or if you bring your own), where you can clean up (or avoid) any fire scars, where the danger of forest fire is low, and where fires are permitted. Finally, keep fires small and contained. A large fire is actually quite inefficient for cooking, and flying sparks from a big blaze are not only a fire hazard, but will burn holes in nearby tents, tarps, and clothing.

For a mound fire, lay down a tarp or ground cloth, cover it with 6 to 8 inches of mineral soil (such as sand or gravel from an area regularly disturbed by flooding), and build the fire. Be sure to scatter the cooled ashes widely away from the campsite. (Photo: ©Alan Kesselheim)

SANITATION

As a matter of general hygiene, especially with a large group, keep a water container (a suspended water bag with a spout is especially handy) near the kitchen, along with a supply of biodegradable soap. That way it's easy for people to wash hands before they cook or eat.

After meals, heat up some dish- and rinse water (boiled rinse water is a good sterilization measure, if you can afford the fuel). Wash dishes 200 feet from camp to minimize any traces of food odor that attract wildlife. If you're using soap (even a biodegradable type), drain the water on unvegetated ground (see the Sanitation section in chapter 1).

Using the Portable Toilet

For a homemade portable toilet, line the container with a heavy-mil plastic garbage bag, and then a second plastic bag. The inner liner is the day's waste container. Each morning securely tie up the inner liner, enclosing the waste, and then leave it inside the bucket or can. Every night add a new second liner. Sprinkle in some bleach powder each day to reduce odor. At the conclusion of the trip, dispose of the waste at a sanctioned disposal site.

People should refrain from peeing in the portable toilet, both to cut down on odors and to minimize liquid content. At some well-used campsites, users are requested to pee on wet sand bordering the water, or right into the water, in an attempt to reduce odors and damage to shorelines.

Showers and Dips

On warm afternoons, a dip in the water is incredibly refreshing and it rinses off the top layer or two of travel grime (for washing etiquette, see the Sanitation section in chapter 1). Beware of sudden dropoffs as you wade in, and of fast current. Swim with a partner if the current is swift.

Portable solar showers are a pretty wonderful boat camp fixture. Fill up the bladder in the morning and drape it on top of your load during the day (if feasible), or fill it as soon as you reach camp. In direct sunlight it won't take long to heat the water (sometimes too hot!). Hang the shower from a high branch or other tie point where it won't drain directly onto vegetation. (A five-gallon bladder will bequeath a half dozen rinses or about three full showers.) If you can't heat the water with solar power, a pot of nearly boiling water, mixed with some cold water, will give you a short shower.

A solar shower is useful for rinsing off accumulated grime and reviving the spirit. (Photo: ©Marypat Zitzer)

CAMP COMFORTS

Sitting Pretty

These days, there is no end of folding camp chairs, inflatable seats, and combination pad/backrest rigs to settle into. The most basic of these are made from foam pads that fold together with reinforcing stays. The two flaps are connected with adjustable straps. Best of all, they're compact enough to pack along even on kayak journeys.

From there, the choices expand to full-length loungers, cushy inflated seats, and the whole gamut of director-style folding chairs, aluminum-tubing picnic furniture, and the rest. Other than your budget, the only limit is how much furniture you're willing to tow along into the wilds.

Portable folding chairs are light and easy to carry, offer support for tired backs, and can supplement a sleeping pad. (Photo: ©Marypat Zitzer)

Zen and the Art of Bug Maintenance

There's something to the business of developing a Zen-like attitude toward insects' existence. Protect yourself as you might, there are still circumstances in which bugs are a hassle. Work to accept them, achieve calmness in their presence, go about your business.

Remember, too, that dawn and dusk are the times of most intense bug activity (especially mosquitoes and no-see-ums). If insect avoidance is a priority, plan your camp routines accordingly.

If nothing else, it is true that bugs are drawn to both heat and motion, so a quiet, cool, and calm demeanor tends not to stir up the insect denizens. Wear long pants and a lightweight long-sleeved shirt (wind pants and jackets work well), tuck your pant legs inside your socks, find a breezy perch, and elevate yourself above the temptation to succumb to bug-induced panic.

Then, if all else fails, retreat to the tent!

SHUTTING DOWN FOR THE DAY

Before you settle completely into relaxation mode, attend to the small details of repair or equipment upkeep. Wet clothes and gear should be hung out to dry (or protected from bad weather). Make note of the things that need attention—a rough spot on your canoe gunwale that should be sanded, the button on your shirt you keep meaning to sew on, that leaky gasket on the fuel bottle. Take care of those details as they come up (or at an opportune quiet moment in camp).

Afternoon and Evening Activities

The memories that stick from outdoor time are, often as not, ones that have nothing to do with the travel or camping routine. That warm afternoon you spent sketching a juniper on the edge of a sandstone rim . . . the secluded side stream you walked up to look for birds . . . an hour of fly-fishing in a pool . . . the streamside talk you had with an old friend. Plan in the flexibility to allow for these; bring along journals, sketch pads, fishing gear, binoculars. Be alert for possibilities and sensitive to your trip mates' needs for solitude.

A deck of playing cards or miniature versions of Scrabble, backgammon, cribbage, chess, and other board games are all easy to stuff in a side pocket and are a fun way to end a day or while away time when

Blackflies and mosquitoes are not usually bad on the water, but if they are, head nets or bug shirts can keep bugs at bay. (Photo: ©Dorcas Miller)

tentbound. An after-dinner round of charades, twenty questions, or minute mysteries can also be hilarious fun, if the mood is right.

When evening settles in, darkness may signal an early bedtime, but it is also a unique segment of the day, complete with its own backcountry rewards. The river ripples past in the distance, a coyote yips from the canyon rim, nighthawks catch insects in the purple twilight, and you can sit back and enjoy it.

Reading. An appropriate reading can expand your awareness of a region's natural and cultural history, illuminate the feats of early explorers, or simply provide a thought-provoking perspective. Try Robert Service or Sigurd Olson in the North Country, John Wesley Powell or Edward Abbey in the Southwest, or Aldo Leopold, Annie Dillard, Joseph Wood Krutch, Henry David Thoreau . . . there is no end of evocative material.

Stargazing. Lie back in the sand and watch the heavens. Unencumbered by city lights, you can pick out the major constellations, find the North Star, identify a planet or two. Simple star charts are an easy way to expand your night-sky knowledge, and several new books cover the legends, stories, and cultural significance associated with constellations. Before you leave town, research whether there are stellar events of interest you might witness. Meteor showers, eclipses, a full moon—all add to the appreciation of night skies and to the memorable moments in the field.

Moonlight paddles. If the light is sufficient and the water is still, there is nothing like a short outing in a boat. Paddle a way offshore, then sit still on the water, look up at the stars, listen through the layers of silence. In the interest of safety, let someone know what you're up to, don't stray far from camp, and (if possible) take a partner along.

Securing Camp

After dinner, and hopefully before it's pitch-dark, take care of the final camp chores.

Camp kitchen. Nest the clean pots and utensils or return them to their stuff sacks, and stash them in the equipment pack. It's best to stow the stove and other cooking paraphernalia, although if the weather is calm and the gear protected, you can sometimes leave things out in preparation for the morning meal. If a tarp is rigged, the group equipment goes underneath, closed up for the night. If you didn't need the tarp, collect all the loose gear in a tight pile and use the tarp to cover it. Tuck in the corners well or weigh them down with ammo cans, water jugs, or loose rocks. Then, if a storm rolls in or winds kick up, you'll rest easy knowing that everything is battened down.

Secure food. Put food away in animal-proof coolers or boxes, or hang it as described in chapter 1.

Last boat check. Take one more stroll through the boat launch site. Check the ropes and knots that hold rafts or canoes. Make sure for the last time that the rafts aren't jostling against anything dangerous. See that any loose gear—personal flotation devices, bailers, sponges—is tucked away inside or underneath boats. Make certain the canoes or kayaks are well above the storm wave line or high-tide zone.

Settling In

In most cases you'll attend to the layout and arrangement of your tent "furniture" before dark. Under duress, you may be forced to arrange the household by flashlight or headlamp.

At night and during inclement weather, make sure that gear is collected under a tarp and that boats are safely stored. (Photo: ©Marypat Zitzer)

Place whatever night necessities you may require close at hand (in the tent storage pocket below a window works best). This collection may include a flashlight, some toilet paper, your reading book or journal, eyeglasses or contact lenses, and drinking water. I also like to have my clothes bag inside (or in a vestibule). Then, in the morning, I can dress for the day's conditions. Even if space is tight, bring in the clothes you want to change into, rain gear, and a jacket.

BREAKING CAMP

Greeting the Day

I've heard dawn referred to as the crack between the worlds. It is, in fact, a very special time of day. If an early departure isn't required, that tranquil window between night and day is a wonderful opportunity to catch up on your journal and sip a cup of coffee, take a walk, sit on the riverbank, or just watch the sun climb above the horizon.

It's best to let that pre-breakfast hour unfold without any rigid expectations. Those who enjoy it by snuggling down in the bag can indulge, while people who prefer to wake up with the birds can do their thing. Imposing an unbending routine on the morning (and messing with your partners' biorhythms) is a recipe for group tension.

Only if it becomes obvious that late put-ins are a consistent problem should the group discuss ways to jump-start the day. One way to allow group members to enjoy their preferred dawn ritual is to rotate the breakfast duty. If real conflict develops over the issue of getting out of camp at a reasonable hour, try alternating early and late starts. In most cases, groups are capable of settling on a comfortable compromise between boot-camp discipline and slug-abed sloth.

Early Starts

Just as alpine starts are sometimes necessary for hikers climbing a high peak (to avoid thunderstorms), an early put-in can be prudent for a paddling party. Generally, dawn is the least windy time of day. When traveling across large open bodies of water, and especially if you want to cross an exposed stretch, early starts make great sense. On trips where afternoon winds have stopped you on previous days, you may want to give up lazy mornings in favor of racking up miles early and then enjoying relaxed afternoons in camp.

Assign the wake-up duty to someone with an alarm on their watch, or to the group member with the most reliable predawn biorhythm. If a sunrise dash is in order, the night before leave the gear organized for quick departure; in the morning, stuff your bag and tent even if they are damp and do away with those treasured morning rituals. You may even want to skip breakfast in favor of a cold cereal and juice stop after you've made your critical crossing.

Leaving the Tent

I get things packed up before I leave the tent. (The only time I don't is when I'm with a slumbering tent mate.) I dress for the day and stow my clothes, roll up my sleeping pad, stuff my sleeping bag (or take it out with me to air), and pack away the flashlight, reading book, and other odds and ends.

As I slip out the door, I leave the clothes bag, sleeping bag, and pad right at the entrance or in the vestibule. That done, I won't have to reenter the tent and track in sand when it comes time to pack up.

If your shoes have been sitting outside, shake them well to dislodge spiders, scorpions, or other night crawlers. On pleasant mornings, take a minute to remove the rain fly. The tent will warm up more quickly with the sun's first heat, and any condensation accumulated overnight can escape. Drape the fly over a bush or rock to dry. Given sufficient time, hang your sleeping bag and liner in the open air so they'll be fresh and dry for the next camp (even in a dry climate, your bag accumulates moisture unless you air it out).

The Breakfast Ritual

Usually the biggest morning decision is whether to have cold (quick) or hot (slower and more elaborate) food to start the day. I find hot breakfasts much more sustaining than cold ones, especially if there's a nip in the air, but I also like the speed and simplicity of cold cereal and dried fruit.

Vary the menu so that you can match conditions. A good compromise is to bake some cinnamon rolls the night before to enjoy on a quick-start morning. Instant hot cereal (cream of wheat, oatmeal, grits) is also a nice option, because all it requires is boiling water.

Organizing for the Day

Each person or set of tent partners deals with their sleeping bags, tent, and clothes. In some cases, it makes sense for tent mates to consolidate their outfit together in a single dry bag or pack. Change into the clothes and shoes you'll wear for the day, and stow the rest in waterproof bags and packs.

A small portion of gear is needed during the day. Put rain gear, a wind shirt, and perhaps a vest inside a small waterproof pack or bag. Pack camera, journal, maps, bug dope, sunscreen, and other ditties in an ammo box or other waterproof case.

The tent, pads, and sleeping bags are bulky enough that they may require a separate pack. Some gear that doesn't have to stay completely dry (sleeping pads, tent poles) can be strapped on the outside of packs or elsewhere in the load.

Dry and air out gear whenever possible. (Photo: ©Alan Kesselheim)

Waterproofing. If you're packing in plastic sacks, leave plenty of space at the top for good closure. Squeeze the excess air out of the bag to reduce volume, and either tie the top in a secure overhand knot or fold the bag down in a series of pleats (at least three or four turns) until it makes a tight, flat seal. If you rely on a roll closure, lay a tent, a second clothes bag, or a sleeping bag on top to keep it closed, and cinch the pack snugly to complete the package. All the plastic bags should be inside packs or stuff sacks to reduce the chance of punctures.

Group gear. Whoever handled the breakfast duties is in the best position to pack up the kitchen and other group gear. Once the dishes are cleaned up, the stove, fuel, pots, cook tarp, and other camp sundries go into the equipment pack or box. Make sure that stoves and fuel bottles are well sealed and free of leaky gaskets. Food goes into coolers or designated packs, protected inside double bags, vacuum-seals, or other waterproofing. The kitchen crew should set aside lunch makings in a hip sack, day pack, or dry bag (or in the top of an accessible cooler). Leave some snack food, energy bars, and powdered drink mix handy as well.

Loading Boats

As camp gets packed up, the focus shifts from kitchen and bedroom to boat and launch site. Carry the packs down close to the boats (if possible, pile them on rocks or grass rather than on sand or dirt).

Before any gear is loaded, attend to the boats. Raft tubes often get soft overnight and need to be pumped up. Any residual sand or dirt should be emptied out of boats. Sponge up puddles of water. Empty the boats of the life vests, paddles, and other loose gear, and organize the tie-down straps or ropes in preparation for the load. Again, canoes and rafts should be at least partially in the water to avoid unnecessary damage to the hull. Kayaks can be onshore but close to the water. Dust away sand and grit from canoe gunwales, raft tubes, and cockpit combings.

One person should oversee the packing ritual so that it goes systematically. As each pack comes aboard, make a habit of brushing sand off the bottom. For rafts and canoes, the bulky items go in first (big packs, coolers, plastic boxes, portable toilet). Try to even the load (boat trim) by centering the heaviest gear or balancing items of equal weight.

Kayaks require just the opposite packing strategy. The smallest packages are shoved far into the bow and stern compartments, followed by elongated luggage (tents, poles, sleeping pads). Finally, the clothes bags and sleeping bags go into the widest sections of the hull. In the case of large-volume tandem kayaks with center hatches, some outsize gear can be fit in (Dutch oven, fire grill, et cetera).

For all craft, the more compact gear goes in next to fill out the corners. Try to make the load snug to avoid shifting in waves or white water. Use smaller packages to pad sharp-cornered objects and protect the hull or tubes. If the load is obviously weighted to one side (or front to back), use the smaller pieces to compensate. Water containers are good for shifting ballast.

Finally, the gear that needs to be handy during the day goes onboard. Personal ditty bags, camera packs, ammo boxes, several water bottles, and lunch all get clipped onto the load with carabiners or stashed in convenient (but out of the paddler's way) spots.

Once the load is in place, lash it down with webbing straps or cord that are secured to D-rings and canoe thwarts. Carabiners or similar clips are handy for fastening smaller gear to pack straps or into the lashing. Gear in kayaks is secured by the hatches and doesn't need to be tied in.

Some tandem kayaks are outfitted with a roomy center hatch, but packing a kayak still requires patience and a certain amount of physical contortion. (Photo: ©Marypat Zitzer)

Adjusting trim. Boats move best when the load is trim. Any list to one side is a daylong bother and should be compensated for, either by shifting gear or arranging the seating so heavier passengers counter-balance the lopsided load. Boats should also be trim in the water from bow to stern. Compensate for mismatched paddler weights by shifting heavy gear to the front or back of the center line.

If anything, load boats so they are slightly stern-heavy. In waves and white water, you won't take on as much water and the boats (especially canoes) are easier to steer. The exception to this rule is upstream travel, when you want the boats to be slightly bow-heavy.

Pulling Apart Camp

When the boats are packed, or while the packing is going on, make a final swing through camp. Look at it as if you are the next camper, just arriving, and hoping for an attractive, unlittered home for the night.

Check the tent sites and kitchen area for any forgotten gear, laundry, or garbage. See that the portable toilet location is tidy. If you used rocks to tie down tent guy lines, put them back where you found them. Sprinkle sand or bits of forest duff over any spots that you manicured for the tent(s) or cooking spot.

Fire sites. If you used a fire, make sure the wood has completely burned to ash, then pour the dead ashes in the water. Scatter the un-burned woodpile along shore or in the forest. In most cases, that takes care of a fire burned in a pan. If you made a fire in a shallow scrape, dispose of the ash with the trowel, stir up the loose sand and make abso-lutely sure the pit is cold, then cover the depression with fresh sand and gravel. Blackened rocks should be thrown into the water or placed, black side down, back in the ground. In designated sites with established fire rings, be sure the fire is completely dead, check for any litter in the coals, and leave unused wood for the next group.

CHAPTER 3

MOUNTAIN BIKING

—

At Home on Wheels

Dennis Coello

IT WAS LATE SEPTEMBER in Colorado's high country. Yellowing aspen and ever-brisker morning temperatures warned of the coming change of seasons, but it was eighty and sunny on that blue-sky afternoon as I sipped coffee in a Crested Butte bakery.

I had pedaled in from Denver, my high-pressure cross-tires (designed for both road and trail) first eating up the paved miles out of the city, and next the good dirt roads which, needlelike, ran between two of the state's 14,000-foot mountains, then up and over the Continental Divide. My hope now was to take 12,000-foot Taylor Pass north of Crested Butte before early snows closed it off until next summer, then drop down the other side into Aspen before heading home. So far I'd been lucky, with only one cold rain and no snowflakes whatsoever during 4 days in the saddle. But then, the weather gods are a capricious bunch.

Fellow mountain bikers stared as I pedaled out of town, for fat-tire bikes are still seldom seen equipped with full panniers and touring kit. Two- or 3-hour fast rides along the trails are the norm, an activity more akin to white-water kayaking than the lazy canoe-trip-down-the-river type of backcountry mountain biking I prefer. Those endorphin-filled trail rides are fun, of course, and sometimes I enjoy them after making a base camp and leaving all my touring gear in the tent. But this time I

Self-supported backcountry mountain bikers above the Flathead River in northern Montana (Photo: ©Dennis Coello)

was looking solely for a final, memorable solo trek to round out a great summer in the saddle. And memorable it was.

I was twisting my way through glacier-scarred Cement Canyon on the hard-packed dirt road when I met up with a jogger. He stopped, asked where I was headed, and then began explaining how to negotiate the maze of forest roads and trails. As a darkening sky and cooler canyon breezes engulfed us, however, he looked up from the topographic map I'd spread across my handlebars. "Look," he said, "it's getting late. Why don't you pedal back to my ranch and spend the night? There's no heat in the guest cabin, but you'll have hot water and a bed."

And so began one of the countless evenings I've spent with strangers in over thirty years of touring. Melville writes that we know life best by its contrasts; two-wheeled touring is exactly that. The jogger and his wife and I drove into Gunnison for a great dinner with conversation, good food, and fine wine. The next night would find me alone in a cold mountain camp, warming my standard soup/rice/jerky concoction and listening to the bugling of elk. And loving that experience as much as the evening before.

I began the next day with the promised hot shower, then pedaled in an unfortunately shaded canyon for one cold hour until I switchbacked into sunlight. Out of the canyon at last, I marveled at the pure green alpine forest, and at towering pyramid-shaped and partially snowclad Italian Mountain (13,378 feet). Plunging off the divide, I rode into a confusion of forest service and old mining roads that required repeated consultations with my compass and maps.

The huge, puffy cumulus of the day before had changed that morning to the warning signs of cirrus, those high wispy clouds against the blue that tell you in high country to be prepared. Thinking I would surely be in Aspen before the flakes, I dawdled, eating lunch with three elk hunters and a woodcutter and snapping pictures of a world whose green and gold colors would soon be pure white.

On the trail from Crested Butte to Aspen before a snowstorm blows in (Photo: ©Dennis Coello)

The question of how soon that would happen began to prey on my mind. Snowflakes borne by a fast wind began to whip about me. Light and insubstantial at first, they melted upon touching ground. But by the time I reached the pass, I needed a compass to find the road.

Have you heard the statement that there's no bad weather, just bad preparation? Well, I was well prepared, and I was learning again how oddly enjoyable the elements can be when you're in them but protected. Granted, my bike weighed far more than those I'd seen back in town, but then the riders of those bikes were back in town as well. I donned another layer, put on my rain gear, and pedaled on.

That night I pitched camp in a white mountain cirque, so high it seemed a million miles from human sounds. Hunger turned my meager food into delicious offerings; fatigue transformed my bag and tent into unbelievable comfort. Shortly before sleep, I closed my book, blew out my candle lantern, and smiled as I thought about the tough riding and sliding ahead on my wet descent into Aspen. Flakes melt, after all. And mud washes off. But good memories remain.

PRETRIP PLANNING

Recent polling of hikers indicates that there are at least two day hikers for every overnight backpacker. When it comes to mountain biking, however, that ratio is probably closer to a thousand to one. A thousand riders, that is, who hit the dirt roads and trails for an hour or two or maybe most of a day, compared to each one who wheels into the backcountry to camp.

Backpackers and thin-tire touring cyclists will tell you that one of the best things about their activities is their escape from the world of managed time. Even far from the workplace, on a day hike or a ride along the trails, our fun is determined by glances at a wristwatch or the digital clock mode on a cycle computer. How often have you wondered if there was time to crest a ridge and have lunch by the lake before turning back? Or if you could pedal a loop a second time and still make it to the car before sundown?

Pack the essentials for spending a night in the wilds, however, for making a simple meal and sleeping warm and dry and bug-free, and you've gone far in returning—even for a short time—to the "natural" pace of life. A weekend away from work provides the opportunity for a 2-day backcountry excursion, an evening spent watching the sun set and the moon rise on the big screen enjoyed by our ancestors. And a morning when you waken slowly to sunlight and birdsong instead of the din of alarm clocks or traffic, or the early Sunday roar of a neighbor's lawn mower. Our species lived this way from day one until the industrial revolution, after all; even a momentary return is restorative. Like H. G. Wells's time machine, your high-tech mountain bike can help leap you across two centuries—backward—once you equip it for overnight travel.

Beyond a reacquaintance with the nighttime sky and a more natural pace of life, however, loading up a bike for travel opens the world to exploration. Gone is the guidebook approach to pedaling, the checking off of each turn made, the constant following of another's suggested path. In their place is the topographic map and compass, and a sense of self-reliance and discovery that far outstrips the usual post-ride blather about who couldn't handle the pace. Speed isn't king in the backcountry.

Transforming a mountain bike into a two-wheeled jeep can give us much, but some things are lost as well. Greatest of all, of course, is the ease of bike handling. No matter how light your food and touring kit, you cannot perform the trail acrobatics possible on a sleek, lightweight, unloaded bike. Riding a loaded bike is more physically taxing, requiring greater lower and upper torso strength for every mile covered.

But remember that what you carry is determined by your in-camp and in-the-saddle comfort levels. You'll soon discover the cost in weight of every item packed, and next time around can jettison the gear that hasn't proved its value. Also, the weight of camping gear and paraphernalia has plummeted over the past decade, as has the weight of bikes. All of which means that, especially for warm-weather rides, which require fewer clothing layers and a far lighter sleeping bag, you can pack for the backcountry with surprisingly little weight and bulk.

Finally, you can always beeline it to a base camp on easy dirt roads and double-track trails, saving the single tracks or steeper jeep roads for a stripped machine. Or you can learn to love the slower speed of loaded travel, the pleasure of no longer seeing the world only as a blur, the opportunity to stop and ditch your bike for occasional on-foot scrambles to sites inaccessible to wheels. Who says life doesn't provide us with options?

It's easy to become lost in arcane tips and a stream of dos and don'ts when reading about mountain-bike touring, and to worry that you'll forget something on the checklist, or, when you at last hit the trail, that you'll do it "wrong." Perhaps, if you think of mountain-bike "travel" instead of touring, it will help you see that this particular kind of backcountry experience is so personal—and nontechnical—that there's scarcely any right or wrong. Traveling on two wheels isn't like whitewater kayaking or downhill skiing. It doesn't require the attention to technique required for successful rock climbing or surfing, or, for that matter, of fast mountain biking on slickrock or single-track. It is instead another way to see the world.

It's wrong, surely, to ride fast around blind corners, to pass folks quickly or too close, to fail to yield to hikers or horses on a trail. And it's wrong—it's illegal—to pedal into designated wilderness areas. But beyond these courtesies and common-sense actions, your "wrong" attempts at backcountry travel will simply make it a bit harder, a bit less enjoyable, than it will be the next time around.

Be careful out there. Be kind to those you meet—human and animal alike—and to the countryside. You're going to have a great time.

Itinerary

Few self-supported mountain-bike rides in the wilds involve large numbers of people. Perhaps this is because relatively few mountain bikers tour, but it is often because, at some point, numbers diminish the experience. Fast-moving 2- or 3-hour rides on a challenging loop, followed by a big-table gathering at a coffee shop, are fun activities for a bunch of friends. On a backcountry tour, more than three or four riders is soon a crowd.

The result of the solo or small-group approach is extremely easy and stress-free pre-ride planning. Unlike canoeing and kayaking, there's no shuttling of cars; you simply turn around when you want to or loop back on dirt or pavement. And with easy access to towns, there's none of the involved computing of food needs and meal prep that goes on before a backpacking trek. Yes, you must make sure your bike and body are in shape, and let people know you won't be around for a while. But after that, there remains only a quick run through the equipment checklist, a stop for food on the way out of town, and a final glance at the map to make sure you can find the trailhead.

Maps. Thin-tire tourers often make do with a motorist's state map, simply avoiding the biggest highways and usually skirting the cities and largest towns. Mountain bikers, however, need more information than provided by "flat" maps (maps that show only linear distance, not the topography).

Why? Well, let's say you'll need 2 days' worth of food to cover the 60 miles of dirt roads and trails between your starting point and the first town you hit for resupply. Let's say too that you know you can handle 30 off-pavement miles per day while fully loaded. Great. But what happens if the terrain between these points is extremely steep? Or if it rains, or if the road- and trail-surface conditions are tougher than expected? You'll make it, of course. (Yet another great thing about mountain-bike touring is that you can always ditch the bike and hike out, then head back for it later.) But what you had planned as an enjoyable wilderness getaway, some fun and aerobic and contemplative time to yourself or shared with some friends, has now become a race against the sun.

A small-scale topo map would have made all the difference. These beauties indicate elevation gain or loss (using contour lines) as well as linear distance. The 7.5-minute series, popular with backpackers and mountain-bike tourers alike, has a "contour interval" of only 40 feet (meaning that hills of any note will appear), and a scale of 1 inch to every 2,000 linear feet along a trail. Unfortunately, at this scale you would have to pack a number of maps on any long tour, and so I study these at home and plan accordingly, taking along only those that cover territory where I might need a navigation aid.

If your route runs through a national forest, you can obtain forest service maps. These are larger in scale than the 7.5-minute topos and lack the topo's contour lines, but possess excellent trail route information and are covered with a ½-inch grid that is helpful in determining distances due to the scale (½ inch equals 1 mile). I study the small-scale topos, and then transfer relevant information onto the forest service maps that I pack along.

And then there are the best-of-both-worlds maps: the waterproof and tearproof maps from Trails Illustrated and the Adventure Cycling

Association, which possess the trails information of a forest service map plus contour lines, as well as occasional larger-scale inset maps, route summaries, helpful tips about the region, addresses for further information, and phone numbers. These waterproof maps are available at many outdoor sport shops, or can be obtained from Trails Illustrated (800-962-1643) or Adventure Cycling (406-721-1776).

Topos are also found at many outdoor sport and bike shops, and can be obtained by writing to: USGS Map Sales, Box 25286, Denver, CO 80225. Forest service maps are sold through forest service offices, but may be purchased before you reach an area (a good idea—all could be sold when you arrive) through the local forest service district office. Consult telephone directory assistance for these numbers, or look under U.S. Department of Agriculture in the white pages and hope you'll find a forest service sublisting.

Food and Water

There are two primary considerations when packing food: Containers must be lightweight and leakproof, to protect panniers and other contents against spills and smears; and you should pack in a way that maintains the integrity of the foodstuffs stowed. Common sense? Yes, but gathering food is often the last thing done before a ride (often on the way out of town), and thus the packing becomes literally a last-minute affair.

Most of us are more concerned with how much food to pack than with how to pack it. Yet poor packing can increase our touring weight (by using too-heavy containers), decrease our food intake (by losing foodstuffs to spillage inside the panniers), and foul our other pannier contents (the leaking of honey, say, from the plastic squeeze bottle container that looked so perfect in the store).

Many outdoor sport stores and catalogs carry tough, see-through plastic jars and bottles of all sizes, with screw-top lids that even the rockiest road or trail cannot knock loose. These containers are sturdy enough to protect the contents, and are sufficiently airtight to discourage raccoons or bears while you sleep. They are also light and last forever. I prefer the softer plastic containers over the hard ones because I can hear the latter hitting against one another. Tiny plastic 35mm film canisters are perfect for packing extremely small items, although those with lids that fit flush with the canister wall will sometimes open by themselves. Needless to say, replace all glass containers with plastic.

Drink up—you'll need more than you think. (Photo: ©Dennis Coello)

While backpackers sometimes carry a week or two of provisions, mountain bikers can cover comparatively long distances quickly and can drop into town for resupply, so they don't need to lug much food along. However, one of my rules is not to shave weight when it comes to food and water (and rain gear, including waterproof gloves and overboots or Gore-Tex socks, and warm clothing). After all, if you're warm, relatively dry, well fed, and well watered, how bad can things really be?

Few bike frames are large enough to mount the cages required to pack enough water for a full day's supply, roughly 320 ounces—eleven large water bottles, or twenty smaller ones. You can, however, pack a quantity sufficient to allow you to travel many miles without taking the time to purify water, or to get you over dry stretches to where water is available.

Most large bike frames have room for three large water bottles, if one is mounted on the underside of the down tube (the tube reaching from the handlebars to the pedals). Shorter frames can usually support only one large bottle on the top of the down tube and a small bottle mounted to the seat tube. (Use sturdy, high-quality metal or plastic cages for backcountry touring.) Additional water can be packed in panniers or carried in leakproof containers on the front rack, or beneath the straps over the tent/sleeping bag/ground pad bundle. Cordura-covered water bottle bags that attach to a rack with four Velcro straps are available. (Note: A one-and-a-half-liter bottle and "bomber cage" is available but, although the capacity is greater, the bottles themselves are made of thin-walled plastic and are thus subject to puncture.)

And then there are the water-bottle-on-your-back "portable hydration systems." A plastic tube sits only inches from the rider's mouth and emanates from a lightweight polyurethane bladder. When bitten, the tube dispenses water, and both hands remain on the handlebars. The original model carried seventy ounces, but other packs now range from smaller-tanked waist belts to eighty-two-ounce back bladders. While these are all the rage with mountain bikers who wish to keep their frames clean of the clutter and extra weight of bottle cages, many tourers prefer to make their bikes do the hauling. Some moved to mountain-bike touring from backpacking, after all, in order to free their shoulders from the strain. For tourers whose small bike frames don't allow enough bottle space, however, and whose racks and packs are full, these water bags are welcome.

Cooking Gear

I cook in and eat out of one small metal pot that's just large enough to contain my stove when I'm packing up. The pot lid is held in place by a web strap, and all is stored inside a stuff sack and buried deep in a pannier. The fuel bottle is sealed in a resealable plastic bag and packed in the same stuff sack as the stove. A pot gripper is invaluable, because the lightest of these backpack pots have no handles.

I prefer a deep, double-walled (insulated) metal or plastic cup for drinking coffee; a single-walled cup (like the famed Sierra cup) for hot liquids will melt a lip. I've used the same thick, durable Lexan-plastic utensils (knife, fork, and soup spoon) for almost two decades. The final item is a small sponge or scrub pad, used with the same biodegradable soap I use to wash myself.

To Tent or Not to Tent

It's always easy to contemplate leaving the tent behind when you're still home, warm and dry and protected from rain and wind and mosquitoes. The 4 or 5 or 6 pounds in your hands seems so heavy. And then, only a few nights later, you're out there beneath a tarp, learning for the very first time what it means for rain to come down horizontally. Or it's two in the morning and you're attempting to find your mosquito repellent in the dark. It must have worn off in the night, you're thinking, or maybe you missed your ears when you were bathing in the stuff 3 hours earlier.

At times like that, you know you'll never hit the woods again without a tent. And, thankfully, manufacturers have been ingenious in designing tents that weigh much less than what we knew as kids. You'll find plenty of information about tents in chapter 1, but I carry my self-supporting, up-in-a-jiffy, last-forever tent only when snow or drumming rain might keep me in it through the day.

For all warm-weather treks I pack, instead, a bivy. A 1-pound bivy is a waterproof sack covering for a sleeping bag, or for you rather than the bag in warmer weather. This lovely alternative in nighttime housing replaces a tent normally four to six times as heavy. There's so little

A mountain biker snug in his bivy sack—biking/hiking boots and stove within easy reach (Photo: ©Dennis Coello)

room you would scarcely wish to spend a day inside one, but for simple sleeping they are great. Some models offer Gore-Tex or other breathable materials that stop rain and dew from coming in, while allowing the water vapor in your breath and perspiration to escape. Almost all have insect nettings, and some are equipped with rods or bands that keep the netting or outer waterproof fabric off your face. Mine is so small that it fits, burritolike, into a pannier. And on summer rides it provides just enough warmth to let me leave my sleeping bag behind. Below 10,000 feet, that is.

But mountain-bike touring does not, like backpacking, mean always sleeping in the out-of-doors. Because the dirt-road (and sometimes paved) sections of our routes take us past fellow humans, merely a spoken request often yields a barn, basement, back porch, or guest bedroom to sleep in. There appears to be something reassuring about people who arrive on bikes; who, after all, would choose two unmotorized wheels as their mode of escape if they had crime on their minds? And so it is common for people to say, "Yes, roll your bag out here or there, and have you eaten yet?" Hospitality is one of the wonderful parts of the history of travel. Making it part of your personal history is only a ride away.

When selecting a sleeping bag and pad, be sure to take weight into consideration. If you go with a self-inflatable ground pad, carry along the tiny patch kit made for these devices; tube patches work best on tubes.

Clothing

Specific tips about shorts, gloves, and shoes appear later in this chapter, but as you are packing you might want to consider including the following items.

A hat of some kind does much to keep you warm in camp when the wind picks up. You don't want to be forced into your tent or bivy sack by cooling weather, and you'll feel silly sitting around in your helmet. A watchcap (no bill) is good to have along in case your head grows cold in the night, and can also fit beneath a helmet for chilly day riding.

Equipping a Bike for Carrying Capacity

Enough of why to load up a mountain bike. Now comes the how. This section covers the two major choices in carrying gear (racks and packs, or trailers) and what to take. There is no one correct way to tour on a

Ready for the backcountry with panniers on one bike and a trailer pulled by another bike (Photo: ©Dennis Coello)

bike, and a few practice runs are required to tailor these suggestions to your body and bike. I also reveal a few boneheaded things I've pulled, to save you the hassle and embarrassment of repeating them. It's best, of course, to learn from experience. But all that experience doesn't have to be your own.

First, if you're thinking of simply tossing all your gear into a back-pack and jumping in the saddle, forget it. Granted, it would be nice to forgo the weight and clutter of luggage racks and saddlebags (panniers), or even the no-clutter weight of a trailer. And if backpacking is your pleasure, your shoulders might already be used to the strain. Biking, however, especially dirt-road and trail biking, requires different move-ments of the upper torso. Hikers move forward, with relatively little shifting side to side. Mountain bikers, on the other hand, are constantly shifting their weight in the saddle. Even if you pare down to the most minimal food and gear, chances are good you'll be chafing from the straps after the first few miles.

Dropping backpacks from the picture leaves three main options: One, a full-on touring kit supported by racks and packs front and rear; two, a lesser-gear setup supported by a single luggage rack over the rear tire, plus two panniers; and three, a trailer. Let's look at each system separately.

Racks and packs front and rear. For the present, at least, and possibly forever, riders with suspension forks cannot mount a front rack. And given mountain biking's move toward ever-lighter, ever-faster machines, designers probably aren't working hard on designing a system that will fit the many fork variations. If your front suspension comes at the handlebars or stem, however, you're in luck—you can mount a front rack and as large a pair of packs as you wish.

Warm-weather backcountry touring makes possible the use of only a rear rack and packs, though it's still not preferable. Why? Between 60 and 70 percent of a rider's weight is supported by the rear wheel; add all

This bike is equipped with front and rear panniers for extensive backcountry travel. (Photo: ©Dennis Coello)

your touring weight in back and you're asking it to handle more than its share. Good rims and axles these days are herculean in their strength, but spokes on the freewheel side of the rear wheel are "dished"—they reach from the rim to the axle at a lesser angle than do the spokes on the opposite side. The straighter the angle, the greater the stress. And thus the greater chance of breaking a spoke.

If you begin your tour with strong, true wheels ("true" wheels roll straight, without wobbling), if you make sure that your tires are inflated sufficiently to handle the extra weight, and if you forgo jumps and wheelies, you'll probably never hear that horrible snap that heralds a spoke's loss of life. But why take the chance that you will be the exception? On your most heavily laden tours (winter rides, multiweek treks), remove some of the weight from the rear wheel by employing a front rack (or trailer—see below), or guarantee against problems by packing the necessaries for permanent or temporary spoke repair. We all know nothing goes wrong when we're prepared for the problem.

So you've got a rigid (non-suspension) fork and are planning to haul a lot of gear. You want the security from spoke problems and the extra storage space provided by a front rack. But which rack? Fortunately, almost any name-brand front rack, when properly mounted, should be strong enough to handle the load and the bashing it will take. It's best if a rack is attached to the fork at its own eyelet (near the axle dropout), and with a bolt long enough to be locknutted on the other side (but not so long that it reaches into the spinning wheel). If space considerations prevent a locknut (or lockwasher and -nut) from being used, employ one of the thread-locking compounds available at most hardware stores. And always, always pack along a spare rack-fixing bolt and nut when on tour. If your fork doesn't provide rack-fixing eyelets at the dropouts, and you are forced to use the around-the-fork metal-in-plastic-housing clamps, be sure the clamp bolts are locked in place (as above) and that you carry a spare as well.

While most racks are tough enough for touring, not all designs are equally suitable. Low-mounting racks, for instance, place the panniers perilously close to the ground; drop into deep ruts or attempt to pedal between rocks or through low brush, and you'll bang up your panniers or pop them off the racks. Besides, low-mounting front racks don't provide

the top-of-rack storage space I prefer for winter touring. It's the perfect place for a figure-eighted spare tire (instructions on how to do this are provided later in this chapter) and a bulky winter parka.

Most of what is true for front racks holds for the rear as well: suspension forces you into considering a trailer, proper mounting is crucial, and high-mounting bags are best. Because the rear rack supports far greater weight than the front, however, its rigidity is even more crucial. Buy the stiffest rack you can find, and don't shave grams—or dollars. There are plenty of other places where doing so doesn't bring with it the possibility of such troubles on the trails—or headaches at night in camp.

Thin-tire tourers considering an escape from the paved world should know this about racks: Full-on, thin-tire touring machines are usually equipped with double eyelets at the dropouts, one for fixing the support arm of a rack, the second for one or two fender support struts. Unfortunately, few mountain bikes offer such luxury, even though mountain bikes, altered slightly to run with high-pressure slicks, higher gears, and full-wrap fenders, are the best urban commuting machine around. Some racks offer fender-fixing points on their support arms, should you wish to mount full-wraps for city commuting (note: remove them when taking your mountain bike into the dirt).

Now to panniers. A trip to even the best-supplied bike shop offers up few of the dozen or more brands available, while most shops carry none at all. Bike magazines guide you toward the phone numbers and addresses necessary to obtain manufacturers' catalogs; books on cycling often have these addresses listed in their appendices. (Thin-tire touring books serve the purpose—many pack makers produce bags for both thin- and fat-tire bikes.) And a library or on-line search should connect you with a recent magazine review of panniers.

The first step, therefore, is to collect catalogs. The second step is to know your requirements for fat-tire touring, and how they differ from those for thin-tire touring. For instance, while the ease and speed of mounting and unmounting a saddlebag is important for thin-tire touring and two-wheeled commuting, a pannier's ability to remain attached to its rack is paramount for mountain biking on the trail. Manufacturers have developed ingenious ways to keep them in place.

A front rack supports small front panniers, a lightweight ground pad, and a sleeping bag to reduce load on the rear wheel. (Photo: ©Dennis Coello)

Another consideration is size and configuration. Some look like overnight backpacks, replete with internal or external pockets and compression straps (the latter for keeping the bag close to the bike frame). Others are comparatively simple drawstring sacks, and still others small, sleek bags that could double well as a biker's in-town attaché case. Although there is little sense in paying extra for a large pannier system if you won't require significant storage space, buying too small precludes a much longer backcountry trek someday.

Some riders split the difference by purchasing medium-size to large rear panniers and a much smaller set for the front. When combined, they are equal to the task of almost any tough trek. When warm-weather single overnights are planned, the smaller bags by themselves—transferred to the rear rack—should be sufficient. And the larger bags by themselves should serve the purpose for around-town shopping and hauling a change of clothes to work or the gym.

No matter which bags you purchase, ensure that the contents remain dry. Keeping spare clothing and your sleeping bag from getting soaked in the wilds can be crucial. Most saddlebags are made of substantial cordura nylon that handles abrasions well and looks of such a tight weave that water could never enter. But it can. Don't leave on tour without rain covers.

Rear rack and packs. Backcountry touring without a front rack and packs is possible, if you are careful not to overload the rear wheel. Long before spokes begin to snap, you'll feel a wobbly, out-of-control sensation. If you do feel this, and cannot or choose not to add a front rack, it's time to do some paring down. A lighter tent, ground pad, or sleeping bag? Fewer tools, clothes, miscellaneous items? A smaller paperback, perhaps, and a less weighty lighting system for reading in the dark?

Unless you are an experienced backpacker or thin-tire tourer, chances are good that until now you've been more concerned with bulk than weight. Considerations change when human muscle must transport it. Long before your first overnight ride, study the equipment checklist provided in this chapter, gather all that you wish to take, spread it before you and look critically at each item. Then ask yourself: Must it go along? Can it be replaced by something lighter that still does the job?

Trailers. While pack builders were busy redesigning their panniers with ever-better attachment systems and pocket arrangements, a couple

Small rear panniers and a lightweight bivy sack instead of a tent are a good setup for tough trails and technical riding. (Photo: ©Dennis Coello)

of novel inventors created their idea of a better mousetrap. Bike trailers have been around for a long time, but this completely new type of trailer enables you to haul your touring load along narrow, bumpy single-track trails. Trailers are the perfect answer for full-suspension riders who wish to hit the backcountry, and they allow the convenience of loading a single, large trailer-mounted duffel bag instead of multiple panniers.

A very heavily loaded rear rack. This Colorado winter ride would have been impossible on thin tires. (Photo: ©Dennis Coello)

Unlike trailers of old, the newest generation are only as wide as your handlebars, attach easily to the bike's rear axle or seat post, and are supported by a single small wheel that tracks nicely as you slither through the woods. The whole thing can be detached quickly once you're in camp, freeing you entirely for unencumbered riding. Wind resistance is negligible because the load sits close to the ground.

And the down side? Well, you'll have to accustom yourself to the "tug" of the trailer, a noticeable feeling when you start off, as is the "dead-ride" sensation you'll experience the first time you board a loaded mountain bike. A second problem, one that rack-and-pack riders escape, is that once your bike's rear wheel has successfully negotiated a tight turn or narrow passage, the trailer must still fit through. A third drawback is the required jockeying of bike and trailer when you're out of the saddle. For a while you'll feel like an eighteen-wheeler when attempting to make a simple turn.

A rider reaches inside a trailer's single cargo bag. (Photo: ©Dennis Coello)

▲ ▲ ▲

Equipment Checklist for Mountain Biking

Few things are as helpful before a ride as a good equipment checklist, but no list of gear fits everyone. The following, however, should at the very least cause you to think of things you might otherwise have forgotten, as well as to mull over what to leave behind.

Amend this list for cold-weather tours, swamp rides, those times when you expect to be in towns a great deal (and wish to be more presentable), and single overnight rides. The quantity of individual items is determined by season, tour length, the load you'll carry, and how often you are prepared to wash clothes by hand.

Cooking Gear
- stove and fuel bottle
- pot with lid
- pot gripper
- plastic cup
- utensils
- sponge or scrub pad

Shelter and Bedding
- tent or bivy sack
- sleeping bag
- ground pad

Clothing
- T-shirts (replaced by wicking, long-sleeve underwear when it's cold)
- long-sleeve shirt or sweatshirt
- hiking shorts and padded briefs (or cycling shorts)
- swim trunks
- undershorts
- long pants (fall and winter tours only, if in towns a lot)
- insulated underwear
- leg warmers or tights
- socks
- cycling shoes or boots
- camp moccasins or sandals
- riding gloves

Foul- and Cold-weather Gear

- shoe covers or overboots
- Gore-Tex socks
- gaiters
- neck gaiter
- ear gaiter
- helmet liner
- stocking cap
- face mask
- gloves
- waterproof overmitts or overgloves
- poncho or chaps or rainsuit
- goggles
- vest
- toe covers (over toeclips)

Personal Gear

- towel
- washcloth
- soap (biodegradable) and soap dish (or plastic bottle)
- toothbrush and case
- floss
- comb
- toilet paper (partial roll)
- deodorant
- shampoo (biodegradable)
- waterless hand cleaner
- nailbrush
- fingernail clipper

Bike Repairs Gear and Tools

Note: Many of the functions performed by the individual tools can be obtained from a lighter-weight multifunction tool.

- tire levers
- spare tube
- patch kit
- Allen wrenches (3, 4, 5, & 6 mm)
- 6-inch crescent (adjustable-end) wrench
- small flat-blade tip screwdriver
- chain rivet tool

- spoke wrench (which fits your spokes)
- channel locks (6-inch handles)
- air gauge
- Schrader tube valve cap (metal kind, with valve-stem remover; only if you are using Schrader valves, of course)
- baling wire (10-inch length; good for temporary repair if something big breaks)
- duct tape (5-foot roll; good for temporary repair if something small breaks, can also be used as tire boot if nothing better is present)
- boot material (large tube patch works well)
- spare chain link
- rear derailleur pulley
- spare nuts and bolts (especially rack-mounting bolts)
- cone wrench
- spare spokes
- tool or tools required to replace spokes on the freewheel side of your hub

Safety and Repair Gear

- helmet
- sunglasses
- pocket knife
- map
- compass
- headlamp and batteries and/or candle lantern and candles
- parachute cord (15 feet)
- ripstop repair tape
- waterproof matches (or kitchen matches in waterproof container)
- pants clips
- thread (heavy-duty) and needle
- panniers and pannier rain covers
- handlebar map bag and/or seat bag
- water bottles
- insect repellent
- whistle
- signal mirror

First-aid Kit

- sunblock
- ibuprofen or aspirin
- butterfly closure bandages
- adhesive bandages
- gauze compress pads (half dozen 4-inch-by-4-inch)
- gauze (one roll)
- elastic bandage or joint wrap
- water purification tablets and/or water filter
- moleskin
- hydrogen peroxide or iodine or Mercurochrome (some kind of antiseptic)
- snakebite kit
- tweezers

Miscellaneous

- book
- notebook
- pen
- trowel (plastic "backpacker's trowel" for burying human waste)

Packing the Bike

Wherever it fits, right? Unfortunately, this is exactly the wrong attitude when balance, wind resistance, and protection of gear are required. Pack hurriedly and you'll pay for it on the trail.

On the matter of weight distribution, thin-tire pavement tourers usually pack two-thirds of the total weight in the rear, one-third in front. (They, like mountain bikers, should of course work toward equal weight side to side.) A full one-third of one's touring weight over the front wheel, however, might work well on dirt roads and relatively tame jeep roads, but will probably be too much for trails. Trail riding requires real maneuverability, and no matter how strong you are in the upper torso, you'll soon tire of lifting a heavy front wheel over obstacles. Shifting just a bit more weight rearward makes a big difference.

Rear rack and panniers. Let's begin with the rear luggage rack. If you're riding with four panniers and your rear panniers are huge, you might have a free pocket large enough for a small sleeping bag. If not, your bag and tent and ground pad must ride where these three largest camping items have ridden since self-supported cycle touring began: mounted on top of the rear rack, parallel with or perpendicular to it. Parallel placement is preferable because it allows easier access to the pannier contents, especially if your panniers are top-loading.

The size of your sleeping bag (stowed inside a durable, absolutely waterproof stuff sack) and tent determines the direction in which you mount these three items to your rack. Cool- and cold-weather tours usually require a sleeping bag so large that there's no room to store either the tent or ground pad alongside it on the rack platform when it's laid parallel to the narrow rack.

When mounting these three items perpendicularly, place the heaviest of the three (usually the tent) closest to the seat tube (the bike frame tube that runs from the saddle to the crankarms), followed by the next heaviest behind it. Then balance the third (usually the ground pad) on top of and between the two items on the rack, and fix all in place with elastic cords or straps. Some mountain-bike tourers prefer webbing straps with side-release buckles, because these can be cinched tightly and won't loosen up on even the rockiest trails.

Trailer. With a trailer, loading the three heavy and usually bulky items—tent, sleeping bag, and sleeping pad—is a no-brainer. Follow the single hard-and-fast rule of bike loading—keep the weight low and close to the frame—and you can't go wrong. You won't need these items until you make camp, so placing all your other gear on top of them in a trailer shouldn't cause any great delay.

Other packs. There are three additional areas—the handlebars, beneath the back of the seat, and in the "triangle" formed by the bike frame's main tubes—where bags can be mounted. In the first two locations, not much weight should be stored due to their height from the ground, and the third cannot bear much volume without restricting leg movement. Nevertheless, these storage areas might prove handy, especially for those wishing to ride with only rear panniers.

Thin-tire touring cyclists use comparatively huge handlebar bags for sunglasses, lip balm, wallet, snack food, camera, handkerchief, keys,

Navigating a narrow bridge over Utah's San Juan River requires that the sleeping bag be mounted parallel to the rear rack. (Photo: ©Dennis Coello)

A sleeping bag and ground pad mounted perpendicularly to the rack
(Photo: ©Dennis Coello)

pen, and a hundred other items that over the miles migrate northward
from their original homes deep inside panniers. This happens because
most thin-tire tourers detach their "bar bags" and pack them inside cafés
or wherever they stop. So much weight at the handlebars isn't a good
idea on pavement, either, but it's an even greater problem on dirt. Choose
instead a small, fold-up map holder with pockets designed for a compass

and energy bar and a number of other small items, but not so much room that you can give in to temptation and make it heavier than you should.

You'll probably find just one bag designed to fit in the open space formed by the triangle of your bike's main frame tubes, so your only considerations will be whether you really require the extra storage and whether you wish to add wind resistance created by hanging a bag there.

Choices abound, however, when it comes to under-the-saddle (or "seat") bags. They range from tiny things barely large enough for a spare tube and a few tools, to huge wedge-shaped affairs designed to hold all one might need on a daylong ride. If you don't have sufficient room elsewhere, and if your frame size is not so small that a seat bag will conflict with your tent or sleeping bag resting on top the rear rack, a medium-size seat bag might be an excellent place for a bulky but light-weight poncho or set of rain gear.

Common sense determines the best place for remaining items. Keep handy (on top) those items either used often (sunglasses and sunblock) or needed quickly (first-aid gear). Note that heavier items settle, and re-member to keep weight low and close to the frame.

A rider in Arkansas's Ouachita Mountains studies a forest service map while making lunch at the trailhead. (Photo: ©Dennis Coello)

A fold-up, handlebar-mounted map holder makes it easy to check where you are. (Photo: ©Dennis Coello)

You'll enjoy your evenings in camp more if the contents of your panniers arrive much like they were when you packed them. Pack food in containers that have screw-top, not flip-top, lids. Make sure oil or synthetic lubricant is in an absolutely leak-proof container. If your panniers have mesh pockets, use them to dry out wet clothing or to segregate unwashed but dirty clothes. If your panniers have no pockets designed for this purpose, air-dry wet clothes by draping them over the tent/sleeping bag/ground pad bundle, holding them in place—securely and away from your spokes—beneath the bungees or webbing. Segregate soiled clothing by packing it in stuff sacks. Fruit takes a beating inside bike bags, so stuff-sack or ziplock even the greenest pears and bananas and the reddest Jonathans. I've slimed many a pannier by thinking a rock-hard piece of fruit could handle the miles.

A final, general packing suggestion is to recall how you leave your bike when taking a break or making camp. You lean it against a tree or large rock, probably. But often you'll end up doing what we all do when riding unloaded: laying the bike down in the dirt—on the non-derailleur (left) side. This is also the side that I most often lay into the dirt when I'm tossed from the saddle. Pack your left-side panniers with things that don't mind getting squished.

Preparing for in-the-Saddle Comfort

Even the most pleasurable backcountry camping experience will not make up for misery in the saddle. And misery—not simple discomfort—will be yours if you fail to take precautions against the pain that can result from the contact points of saddle, hands, and feet. These precautions come in two forms: the proper shorts, gloves, and shoes to insulate your body from contact with the bike, and a "sport-specific" training program designed to accustom your body to the extra strains of touring.

Shorts and saddles. Given enough time in the saddle, you could ride without padded shorts very comfortably. I once began an around-the-world ride on a brand-new rock-hard leather saddle, pedaling in non-padded shorts, and cried my way across the first two states. By the end of that ride, however, my rump had toughened so much that I could have replaced the now-worn saddle with a new one—or a cement block—and scarcely noticed it.

A backcountry face-off with a thirsty cow at a Utah livestock water tank
(Photo: ©Dennis Coello)

Padded shorts, a well-used saddle, and a rear end used to the trails all
help you to avoid pain in the derriere. But if you set out for a weeklong
loaded mountain-bike tour and all your pedaled miles (even a great number of miles) thus far have been unloaded, you'll be sleeping on your
stomach for the first three nights. Loads—whether packed in panniers or
a trailer—cause us to work harder for every mile. And while you might
be out of the saddle when pulling the occasional tough hill, most of the
time you will be pushing against the leather between your legs.

Padded bike shorts make sense even in the boonies, but Lycra is a
tougher call. I prefer padded briefs worn beneath canvas hiking shorts.
Pockets are handy when you're not in the saddle. Besides, hiking shorts
are more comfortable when you're hiking (away from camp or when you
ditch your bike to scramble to an overlook or through brambles to a
creek), and you won't look like a bike geek to the townspeople when you
drop out of the mountains or come in from the swamps for a momentary
taste of civilization and resupply.

Gloves and handlebars. You'll be pulling on your handlebars. This is one reason why upper torso strength is required, and why your neck, shoulders, and forearms feel the strain. Hands can also take a beating off pavement. The thinly padded fingerless bike gloves worn by most cyclists are fine if you're riding with fork or handlebar-and-stem suspension and they are preferable for gaining a good feel for the trail. If you're not suspended, however, you'll have to make up for it with the softest (but durable) handlebar grips you can find, plus gloves with somewhat thicker padding. Remember, touring puts your hands in contact with the bars for hours and hours, day after day.

Thin-tire tourers sometimes experience a going-to-sleep tingling sensation in the two outside fingers on each hand, especially if the padding on their gloves is insufficient and if they fail to alter their hand position. Backcountry mountain-bike tourers are usually off their bikes much more often than their pavement-bound cousins, but finger numbness can still result. Equipping your bike with "bar ends"—those ingenious and lightweight hollow metal tubes that clamp onto the end of your handlebars and provide for additional hand placement—not only helps alleviate this problem, but increases climbing power dramatically. Short bar ends are ideal for fast, stripped-bike trail riding, but the long, curved models allow tourers to stretch out on fast-riding dirt roads, and provide an additional position for the hands.

Shoes and pedals. Footwear is another area in which self-supported tourers often differ from the larger mountain-biking crowd. Toeclips and straps are usually preferred, for example, over the click-in, cleat-locking pedals. Click-ins might be more efficient when tested in performance labs, but this is a world apart from the wilds. Mountain-bike "boots" equipped with cleats have been developed to provide the best of both worlds: pedaling efficiency, plus traction and comfort when hiking. Unfortunately, mud and rocks occasionally find their way into boot cleats and prevent engagement with the pedal clips.

Do not be surprised if the shoes you cycle in quite comfortably when pedaling unloaded are insufficiently stiff for loaded touring. The reason is, again, the additional power that must be exerted to cover the same ground with additional weight. Older riders, especially, whose feet have stretched with age (a normal occurrence due to the flattening of the arch), might require in-shoe orthotics to provide the necessary support.

Off-pavement tourers who choose non-bike shoes usually prefer low-cut (below the ankle) hiking boots that meet the following requirements: a very stiff mid-sole, to reduce pedal strain on the instep muscles; a tread that is sufficiently aggressive to allow for good traction when pushing the bike, yet not so ribbed or corrugated that it causes great difficulty getting into and out of the toeclips and straps; a wide, stiff toe box that will not compress after hours of pressure against the clips (thereby causing pain to the toes); and all-day comfort in and out of the saddle.

Fenders. Full-wrap fenders are not the best way to go in dirt, because mud and snow quickly pack up between the tire and fender and stop you cold. Very short fenders (requiring no support arms) and platform racks (in which the top of the rear rack is solid) work fairly well to catch the muck intent on flinging itself onto your back. In front, any number of down-tube-mounted splash guards help to protect your feet and legs.

Gearing. A final in-the-saddle comfort consideration is ease of pedaling. In short, while wide-ranging gears make your derailleur perform slightly less snappily, loaded touring makes you appreciate the ability to pedal very slowly up long or steep climbs (derived from very low gears), and also to pedal higher gears when flat or downhill smooth dirt roads allow you to take advantage of the increased speed provided by your additional touring weight. Higher gears are also a must when you switch to slicks (treadless tires) and use your mountain bike for commuting. Gear ranges from the low 20s (in gear inches) and even lower, to 100 and above, are easily obtained through freewheel and chainring alterations.

Tire traction. Specialization in tire manufacture seems to be the rule, allowing ever-faster travel in particular conditions with one particular tire. The rub is that fat-tire touring often puts us in contact with greatly varying conditions, and as a result we are presented with a choice: select a multipurpose, variable-pressure tire that handles all conditions somewhat well, or be willing to pedal inefficiently on those surfaces encountered over the fewest number of miles. If you've got tough, steep trails ahead of you for the most part, it might be best to use whichever tires provide the greatest amount of traction in the dirt.

No matter what kind of tire you choose, it is essential to pack a spare, or at the very least a good "booting" material ("boots" are used inside a tire to plug a hole in the sidewall or tire casing), along with a spare tube

Think in terms of traction *and* protection when choosing tires. Tire liners—thin plastic strips that mount between the tire and tube—are a good idea for desert trails. (Photo: ©Dennis Coello)

and patch kit and pump. If you choose to carry a spare tire, it is essential to fold it correctly to avoid crimping the thin wire bead that runs along the two inside lips, the portion of the tire that clinches to the wheel.

Folding a Tire

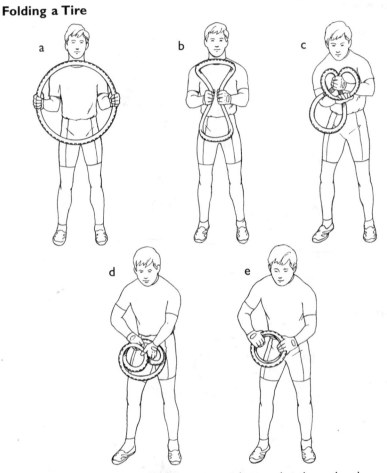

a. Begin by holding the tire before you, with your hands at the three o'clock and nine o'clock positions.

b. Now bring your hands together, toward your chest, creating two long, narrow ovals, one above and one below your hands.

c. Next, take hold of both sides of the tire with your left hand, and with your right hand reach through the lower loop toward the upper loop. Take hold of the upper loop and pull it down toward your left hand, which is still holding both sides of the tire at your chest.

d. As you bring this upper loop downward, notice that you've created two additional, smaller loops.

e. Gradually release the grip of your left hand and fold these smaller loops down upon one another. You now have four small circles of tire, all running in the same direction. Use tape or twine—or two spare toeclip straps—to hold the tire in place.

▲ ▲ ▲

Mountain Biking Etiquette

It's no secret that there has been friction between bicyclists and other users of the backcountry, and the burden is on us bicyclists to make ourselves good guests and equal users. The International Mountain Bicycling Association has issued these guidelines to resolve questions about right-of-way and trail use.

Remember that mountain bikes are not allowed in federal wilderness areas, most national parks, and some regional and state parks. Check before you go.

- Ride on open trails only.
- Leave no trace.
- Control your bicycle.
- Always yield the trail (whether to hikers or people traveling by horse).
- Never scare animals (domestic or wild).
- Plan ahead.
- Observe all rules and regulations.
- Stay on designated trails.
- Be alert and courteous.
- Avoid muddy areas.

SETTING UP CAMP

In his book *Deliverance*, James Dickey describes setting up camp as "colonizing" the place. It's what humans on the move have been doing throughout the ages: scanning their surroundings when they tire and the sun sits low in the sky, searching for that flat, protected patch of ground where they can eat and sleep in peace. This continuity of action, this elemental link with our forebears, should put you in touch on some deep reflective level with all the sandaled and moccasined and booted wanderers and explorers and armies who have gone before. You'll be too busy, of course, to reflect on this while erecting your tent and cooking dinner. But later, as the moon and night sounds rise and you rest on an elbow looking into the gathering dark, you'll have time to think. This is, after all, but another of the experiences that backcountry touring is all about.

This biker has ridden dirt roads and trails to the border of Arkansas's Upper Buffalo Wilderness Area, hidden the bike in the woods, and hiked to Hawk's Bill Crag to spend the night. (Photo: ©Dennis Coello)

It has always been my belief that backpackers spend so much of their time planning for and making camp precisely because lugging a huge pack is such a comparative pain. Mountain-bike tourers, in contrast, view the countryside unencumbered. Not tethered to a load, they can at a whim leave the saddle to smell the flowers. Many riders take this end-of-day opportunity to toss their panniers inside the tent and head out again on stripped bikes, or to hike off into the woods with only a day pack.

In short, riding is so enjoyable that mountain bikers relegate making camp to the necessity that it is. They still need the proper food and gear to ensure sustenance and a good sleep, and to choose a safe and quiet campsite. But cyclists, more akin perhaps to those earlier meanderers for whom travel in the wilds emphasized the travel, tend to spend less time in camp than backpackers, and thus dwell on it far less.

Arrival in Camp

My habit is first to set up my stove for a cup of coffee. (If instead I plan to make a fire, or to forgo cooking entirely for the night, I proceed at once to erect my tent or lay out my bivy, roll out my ground pad, and fluff out my sleeping bag.) Next comes the daily sprucing up, a quick one-water-bottle ablution performed in what at home would be termed sink-bath style, and with a second bottle I wash out that day's T-shirt, socks, and shorts. I'm usually sipping a cup of delicious black coffee by the time I begin to wash, two activities whose individual pleasure quotients more than double when combined. The coffee also assuages the displeasure of washing dirty clothes.

A rider unpacks his sleeping bag shortly after making camp, allowing it to regain its loft before nightfall. (Photo: ©Dennis Coello)

Dressing for Camp Comfort

Then I don a clean T-shirt (or long-sleeve wickable undershirt, depending on the season) and shorts, get dressed once again in whatever I'll be wearing to ward off the bugs or cold during dinner, trade my cycling boots for moccasins, and pull from my panniers the food and cooking supplies, and locate my headlamp before I'm forced to root around for it in the dark (I also pack a candle lantern and spare candles for reading on long rides). It sounds like a lot, but the time involved since leaving the saddle is a half hour, tops.

THE CAMP KITCHEN

For tips on setting up the camp kitchen, refer to chapter 1.

Stoves

While mountain bikers have the advantage of not having to carry much spare fuel (due to little use of the stove, plus access to towns), they should consider how readily available their particular fuel might be in hoped-for resupply points, and also the size containers they might be forced to purchase and resultant wastage.

Remember that mountain-biking gear gets bounced around a lot; the effect on poorly packed stoves and extra fuel supplies can be deadly. Be absolutely sure your packing guards against breakage and fuel leaks. Also, because bikers tend to use their stoves less frequently, it is easier to arrive in the backcountry with one that refuses to work. Just because it roared into action the last time you used it three trips ago does not mean it will quit its sputterings next time. Crank it up before you hit the trail.

Matches

Matches are like stoves: When you need one, you need it to work. I've always found that "waterproof" matches work best when I've packed them in such a way that they won't get wet, or at least not soaked. For years I've trimmed them to fit inside a 35mm film canister, half the heads pointed one way, half the other so that more will fit. Do not throw kitchen matches willy-nilly into your bags, however, for their strike-anywhere capability means exactly that.

Food

Not just armies travel on their stomachs. Tasty food on a biking tour, especially when you're working hard, is a real spirit-lifting treat;

nourishing food, and good quantities of it, is a physiological require-
ment. Mountain bikers tend to pack the fresh foods they like most and
that travel well.

After you've set up camp, it's time for dinner. My expedient routine
is to boil a couple cups of water, toss in two handfuls of instant rice, add
a half box of instant soup and a few ounces of beef, chicken, deer, or elk
jerky, and let it all cook for about 5 minutes. My fellow bikers for the
most part follow this fast one-pot approach, but their preferences seem
to be the instant pasta bags. These require 8 to 10 minutes of boiling, and
taste fine without the suggested half cup of milk (save it for the granola)
or butter.

Strive to keep food and food smells out of the tent in bear country.
See chapter 1 for details.

SANITATION

For the things you need to know about disposing of wastes, see chapter 1.

CAMP COMFORTS

Hard-riding (and therefore tired) touring cyclists require few things to
be comfortable in camp. If they have enough food and water, if they can
free themselves of insects (through repellent or clothing), and have
brought enough layers (and hat and gloves) to be warm, comfort and a
good sleep are ensured.

There is one item that has of late greatly increased my comfort in
camp: the portable chair. These lightweight devices (the lightest I've
seen weighs a mere 10 ounces) combine with a ground pad (inflatable or
non-) to provide a padded seat and wonderful backrest that's great when
eating, reading, and just lounging. When not in use, the chair rolls up
and can be carried in a pannier or on the rear rack. Be sure to protect it
from burning embers, which can melt a hole in its nylon pad or, even
worse, in your ground pad.

SHUTTING DOWN FOR THE DAY

Securing Your Bike

If you aren't alone in camp or are alone but not far from civilization,
attach your bike to the tent by threading an elastic cord or web strap
between some spokes, then securing the other end to a guy line. Do this
in such a way that it's unnoticeable at a glance, especially to someone

who might have only a flashlight for assistance. Or do so twice, once so that it's very noticeable, the second time so it's hidden. People dopey enough to steal will still be congratulating themselves for freeing the obvious connection right about the time you wake up and scare them with a yell. In more than thirty years of touring, the only time I've been hassled in my tent was in a field in Ireland. The culprit's tug came at the tent-front guy line, and when I unzipped the flap to leap out at him, I sat looking—face to face—at a cow.

BREAKING CAMP

Breakfast

Granola (packed first inside freezer-strength resealable bags, then inside small stuff sacks) is the favorite for warm-weather breakfasts, served in a bowl and sprinkled liberally with powdered milk. One good water-bottle dousing and you're ready to eat. The stove is cranked up for coffee or, if there's a fire, the person who made it has of course had a pot of water on since the first flame. Instant oats and honey is the standard cold-weather wake-up meal.

The ultimate in camp comfort is a lightweight, easy-to-pack chair. (Photo: ©Dennis Coello)

A full moon in the Wasatch Mountains of Utah (Photo: ©Dennis Coello)

Packing for the Day's Ride

Long before they hit the backcountry, most bikers know the amount of food required to sustain them on a single day of trail riding. Well, increase it, especially the snacks. Most energy bars are very filling, as well as nutritious and convenient to carry, and can even substitute as a meal if you've counted on reaching a town but are held up. Pack your lunch and snacks so they're accessible; augment them when you pass by a store.

Ruth Gorge, Denali National Park, Alaska (Photo: ©John Harlin)

CHAPTER 4

SKIING AND SNOWSHOEING
—

At Home on a Winter Track

John Harlin

WHEN I THINK BACK to my winter camping experiences, it's rarely the nights in camp that come to mind. Almost invariably, daytime images flood my memory. Skiing, climbing, observing—these are the things that draw me to the winter landscape. At night I cook dinner, read, and sleep. Occasional nocturnal events stand out, like the time high on a Peruvian peak when wind blew the dome tent so horizontal that I worried about smothering in its nylon. Or the time in Rocky Mountain National Park when I awoke in the middle of a subzero night in a fit of claustrophobia brought on by my excessively warm triple-bag system. But I'm seriously hard-pressed to find camps that were nearly as memorable as the day's events. And, come to think of it, that's the way I like it.

Spend a few nights camping in the snow, and the whole process, which once might have been intimidating, becomes second nature. You'll look back, as I do, at a multiday ski tour in Colorado and think of the aspen glades, the bizarre snow sculptures piled high on trees, your dog's joy in bounding through the snow. Camp? Yeah, I guess I must have done that. Why else would I have hauled that sled? But the specific after-dark activities blend in with so many other nights in a tent that I can't for the life of me recall the circumstances. When I do think of a glorious camp,

I remember it for the scenery, for how the warm morning sun traveled slowly down the hillside while I watched cocooned in my bag until its rays touched my tent like a magic wand. Because of the long nights, winter camping isn't something you generally do for its own sake; you do it as a vehicle to bring you and keep you outside at a glorious, underappreciated time of year.

PRETRIP PLANNING

Winter can easily seem like an uninspiring time to go camping. The days are short and harsh, the nights long and cold, the gear heavy and expensive. But there are compensations. More often than not, you'll have the backcountry to yourself and the wilds feel much wilder than they do in summer. Snow is a purifying elixir; those white crystals make magic with the landscape, metamorphosing trees into sculptures, turning the very air into a sparkling, crackling substance. Midwinter days rarely feel harsh if you've clothed yourself to suit the climate. Appropriately attired and mentally adjusted, you'll be able to shrug off wind and cold. You might not choose to head out in a storm, but if one comes your way, you'll find it an interesting adventure, rarely something to fret about.

Long nights can't be denied—but they can be enjoyed. If you're a reader, you can revel in a long book, free from distraction. Relaxed, unpressured conversations with your tent mate(s) can be enormously satisfying. And, more than likely, you'll find that sleep comes easy, long, and restful.

You could also head out in the springtime, when the days are stretched and relatively warm. Spring in snow country varies widely in its timing—typically from March to May, sometimes June in the higher mountains. Occasionally "winter's" biggest snowfall arrives in the spring, so you can't take the season lightly. But more often than not, you'll find spring offers the purity, beauty, and solitude of the snow season, charmed by friendlier days.

Praising the joys of snowy-weather camping is easy to do from a distance, but I know how hard it can be to motivate once you're in the grip of winter. This is a season when most of us are looking for ways to pamper ourselves, not walk an icy gauntlet. In winter, getting out the door requires a leap of faith, a trust that what feels like folly will turn out to have been worth the effort. Some of us have learned, through experience, how great are the rewards of snow camping. Only through your personal experiences will you find out if these rewards are right for you.

Itinerary

The most odious part of planning your summer "wilderness" trip often is making sure you have the necessary permits and backcountry reservations. For some destinations, you need to get those permits six months in advance. In the winter, however, permits are rarely booked up, rarely even required. Still, it's a good idea to call the regional management agency for hints on local conditions. If the rangers seem as though they are trying to scare you out of winter camping, don't take them too seriously. But these warnings are worth hearing even if you're an experienced winter camper. Pay special attention to advisories about avalanche danger. Rangers might also warn you about notorious windiness, local cold pockets, or partially frozen streams and lakes. If there isn't a local recreation manager to help you out, read the guidebooks well and study the topo maps. Try to learn about winter camping in a relatively benign environment.

Other than that, trip planning in winter is about the same as in summer. But do remember that you probably won't travel nearly as many miles in a day as you might expect. How fast and far you can travel depends on large variables such as the depth and stickiness of the snow, whether you're traveling by snowshoes or skis, the hilliness of the terrain, whether you're wearing a pack or hauling a sled, your skill level, and your conditioning. If you're following a trail that's mostly downhill and you're on skis, you could go tens of miles in a day. But if snow falls that night, it might take you several days to cover the same distance coming home. Breaking trail, you'll go no faster than 1 mile per hour and probably closer to 0.5 mile per hour. Allow yourself plenty of time before dark for basic camp chores, like setting up the tent and finding water. You can always go skiing or snowshoeing around camp if you have extra time—just be sure to bring your map, compass, and emergency gear in case you have trouble finding your way back to the tent. Don't take any chances when you're away from your tent, sleeping bag, and stove.

Once snow hits the ground, our lives depend on our equipment. So read carefully through the Equipment Checklist for Snow Camping in this chapter and refer to it every time you pack your bags. A single missing item can ruin a winter's outing, perhaps even endanger you and your partners.

Food and Water

A few things distinguish winter cooking from summer cooking. You'll almost always be making dinner in the dark. You'll be extraordinarily tempted to cook in the tent. You might not find any liquid water. Your stove might sputter in the cold. And you'll be even hungrier than usual. None of these obstacles are hard to overcome, at least not with a little forethought. Without proper planning, however, you're in for unpleasant times, especially because you need to take in lots of calories to compensate for those you're burning to stay warm.

The good news is that you can eat all the calories you want—pile on the butter. The bad news: You have to carry all that food. In my opinion, the only serious food considerations are to bring more fatty food than you otherwise would (it won't spoil), bring plenty of hot drinks like hot chocolate and herbal tea (the caffeine in coffee will make you pee and require you to melt more snow), and, above all, bring lots of food.

For lunch you'll want things that don't freeze solid. Certain energy bars will break your teeth. Eat a hearty breakfast and keep on chowing all day long. Eat a good dinner, then snack again before going to sleep. I think all this eating is a wonderful thing.

I've heard that in places it gets so cold that boiling water poured from a teakettle freezes before it hits the ground. That kind of cold is beyond my experience, but I do know that hot food cools quickly when snow camping, which is why most winter campers prefer insulated mugs. If you have room, bring an oversized mug for food, and a regular (or oversized) one for drink; that way, you can eat and drink simultaneously. If you don't have room, bring the larger one and you can eat out of it, scrub it with snow, then drink your hot beverage. Or bring a plastic bowl, but make it a tough rubbery model that won't crack in the cold. Metal plates drain heat way too fast. Or eat from a group pot, which you can periodically warm on the stove if you're careful not to burn the contents. You can buy thermal wraps for water bottles; you can also make them yourself by cutting up an old closed-cell foam pad and duct-taping or neoprene-gluing a wrap.

Winter Tents

Tents are rated by their seasonality, the vast majority being "three-season"—spring through fall. A "four-season" tent distinguishes itself primarily by its ability to withstand heavy wind and snow loads. You can use your three-season tent in the winter if you're camping someplace where wind and deep, heavy snow won't be a problem. Make sure it seals up particularly well—no uncovered panels of mosquito netting that allow breezes or, worse, spindrift to fill the tent. Pick one that's roomy enough to accommodate your gear and bulky sleeping bags, and to allow plenty of sit-up space for you and your partner(s) while you eat, dress, stretch, and play board (bored) games. It's ideal to use a tent rated for one person more than will be on the trip—i.e., a three-person tent for two people, et cetera. The additional bulk and weight of such a tent often is worth the trouble for the extra room it affords. Most such voluminous tents are freestanding. Freestanding tents are certainly easier to erect in the snow, where staking-out can be a tricky affair.

Dome tents are perennial favorites of winter campers because of their internal volume and because they typically withstand the wind quite well. Dome or otherwise, the more poles the tent has and the more they cross each other, the better the tent should be at resisting adverse conditions. Another thing to look for is steep walls that shed snow. Avoid tents with big unsupported spans of low-angle cloth. These collect snow and collapse. Vestibules have become increasingly common on tents and are now considered almost essential to winter camping. This is the perfect place to cook if you have to do it in your shelter. It's also the spot to leave wet packs, boots, and clothing.

Huts

This book is about camping, but what you really care about is experiencing the winter wilderness, right? It's not the nylon walls at night that make your experience great, but what you do by day—and the fact that you're spending day after day out in the backcountry. So consider

Snow campers like their tents to have steep walls so that snow slides down instead of piling on. (Photo: ©John Harlin)

using huts, at least on occasion.

These come in all shapes and sizes, some with caretakers, others where you're on your own. If you don't become addicted to huts, you'll certainly find these to be a superb transition to the full winter camping experience—a way to get your feet wet, as it were, in a place where you can dry them back out again. There are hut systems in the United States, most notably Colorado's Tenth Mountain Trail complex. Canada has quite a few more, many of which are reached by helicopter and used as a home base for further exploration, generally on skis. Be forewarned, however, that the best huts are usually booked far in advance. Make your reservation six months to a year in advance.

Winter recreation and huts go together like peanut butter and jelly. They allow you to stay outside day after day and be warm and social at night in a roomy environment that has all the necessities of home. Sharing a cabin, however, does require you to practice consideration for your fellow hut dwellers. (Photo: ©John Harlin)

Winter Sleeping Gear

Sleeping bags, as you know, are rated by minimum temperatures. But these ratings are rough guidelines at best. For one, the industry is just beginning to standardize its rating system, which means one company's minus-10-degree bag won't keep you as warm as another's. Equally important, individuals' physiologies vary so widely that no standardized system will ever tell you exactly what you need.

But you can have a pretty good idea just based on how you normally sleep. Do you have the home comforter stacked high, while your mate sweats under light sheets? Then get a bag rated to 10 or even 20 degrees colder than you ever expect to experience. Do be sure that your bag is suited to the occasion. The winter camping habit requires a fairly hefty investment in specialized—and expensive—equipment, not least of which is the sleeping bag. Fortunately, there are ways to improvise while you're getting started.

For economy, you can layer two bags together. Either buy an overbag designed extra-wide to fit over your normal three-season sleeping bag, or find an inexpensive summer-weight bag that zips fully open. If your three-season bag is roomy enough to accommodate the lightweight bag inside, do that. But if you find yourself squished tight inside, you're better off unzipping the summer bag and draping it over your regular bag. You and your partner might even share in this cover, thus sharing some of each other's heat as well. But if you use the overbag as a comforter, you'll find yourself battling cold spots, as well as carrying the extra bulk. So in the long run you'll want to get a real winter bag.

Another option is to wear a bivy bag over your sleeping bag even inside the tent. This gives you a few extra degrees of comfort, maybe enough to meet your needs. You can even combine the bivy bag with the three-season bag and an overbag. Do whatever it takes to stay warm.

Winter bags are available with ratings so chilly-looking that you'll get frostbite just reading the label. If you're camping in heavy-duty cold, invest in something that will take you to minus 20 or even minus 30 degrees. But if your snow outings will take place in milder climes or late in the snow season, you can get by with something closer to the 0-degree rating. Your trade-offs with an extremely low-temperature-rated bag are extra weight and bulk, and a more limited season wherein the bag is useful. Consider what you're using for spring through fall, and buy a winter bag that takes over from that temperature range down to what you'll reasonably expect to encounter, depending on where you live or vacation.

Synthetic sleeping bags are making great strides toward catching up with goose down, and it seems that a new fiber—Polarguard 3D—is showing promise in terms of being lightweight, compressing well, and being durable (retaining its loft over the years). But a serious winter bag uses so much fill that you'll really want to minimize weight and bulk—and maximize longevity. Also, in true snow camping conditions, you shouldn't have to worry about your bag getting wet. All this means that most indicators point toward goose down as the fill of choice; 700 fill weight is ideal for great loft without an extravagant price tag (fill weight refers to the cubic inches that 1 ounce of down will occupy under controlled laboratory conditions).

Seriously consider a synthetic bag only if you live in country where wet conditions frequently invade the winter season—places like the Pacific Northwest and New England. But whenever the climate is that wet, your normal three-season bag might suffice with a little extra clothing inside. If you're concerned about your bag getting wet, consider buying a three-season model with a water-resistant/breathable shell. Such a shell adds considerably to the versatility of your bag, especially if you like to occasionally sleep under the stars or in a snow cave.

In addition to quality goose down, you'll need a bag with a draft collar that snugs around your neck and shoulders. As the name implies, the collar slows air leakage through the hood. And you'll want a hood that draws around the face, leaving your mouth exposed but the rest of your head covered. What's more, the hood should stay in that position on your face even as you toss and turn. Such a characteristic is partly dependent on the quality of construction and partly on matching the design to your physique. So be sure to try out the bag in a store, cinching it tight and rolling around on the floor. Don't buy a bag that's too wide, because excess interior volume is just wasted space that your body has to heat and where drafts can circulate. But don't make it so snug that you can't wear some clothing inside should you want to. I use a long version of my bag (for people taller than me) just to give myself room to store my boots inside. Most people don't do this, so I present it as a consideration, not a suggestion.

There is a considerable science devoted to sleeping bag manufacturing, and competing companies will subject you to a bewildering array of features. If you're buying from a reputable company, you don't have to worry about all these details. Check with your retailer for his or her opinion on how conservative a sleeping bag manufacturer is with its minimum temperature ratings. Women tend to sleep colder than men do, so if you can find a woman who is an experienced winter camper (alas, a rare breed), trust her judgment on bag ratings, especially if you're female yourself. Then compare weight, how well the bag fits, how the hood cinches around your face (and how well it stays there when you roll), and price.

Vapor barrier liners, or VBLs, are moisture barriers worn close to the skin. They can be bag-shaped liners in sleeping bags or clothing-shaped garments worn under your insulating layers of clothing. The VBL concept is multifold. Body-generated moisture (perspiration, generally insensible while you're sleeping) carries with it considerable heat. If you keep this moisture from traveling out of your bag, you've also hung onto quite a few calories. Also, because all this moisture is moving through your bag, it's inevitable that a little of it will be gradually absorbed into the sleeping bag's insulation. This can be especially true in a very thick winter sleeping bag, because the insulation could be so good that the outermost layers of the bag are cool even though you're toasty warm inside. When your body's moisture reaches this cool zone, it might condense, maybe even freeze. In any case, the insulation gradually becomes less insulative. VBLs prevent this from happening. Lastly, most human bodies will put out insensible perspiration until the ambient humidity reaches a certain level, after which no additional moisture is generated. So in a VBL, you get wet to a certain point and that's it.

Getting wet is what people don't like about the VBL concept. To reduce that clammy feeling from trapped perspiration, wear a thin layer of synthetic long underwear (top and bottoms). Still, some people don't stop perspiring no matter the ambient humidity; others can't stand any sense of moisture near the skin. But if you can tolerate the slightly clammy feeling, a relatively inexpensive VBL lowers the temperature rating of your bag by 10 or more degrees. I've only used the sacklike bag liners, and they have worked for me, but I've heard that VBL clothing works even better. This makes sense because it keeps the vapor barrier layer closer to your skin. It also seems like a better system because you could use the VBL clothing during the day.

But be warned that perspiration due to exertion will not shut down even after you've reached humidity saturation. If your winter travels elevate your heart rate while you're wearing VBL clothing, you could find water cascading down your flesh. That doesn't feel good, and it feels even worse when you stop and all that water starts to cool. Unless you're ice fishing or doing some other sedentary activity, leave the VBL for the sleeping hours.

Thermal pads. Even the warmest sleeping bag compresses under your body, leaving you with precious little insulation in the most cold-conductive spots. Insulating yourself from the snow below is, in fact, at least as vital as insulating yourself from the cold air above. The best system is to carry three pads for a party of two. Each person can sleep on a self-inflating pad. The third pad should be a closed-cell foam variety that can cover the exposed floor if you've brought an oversized tent. You could use this pad for sitting on outside, for cooking on inside in an emergency, to slip under the pad of someone who feels chilled at night, and as a hedge against a leaky inflatable.

Three-quarter-length pads are popular among summer campers, but aren't so hot for snow camping because you have to pile extra clothing, jackets, et cetera, under your feet. Also, if you spill a pot or otherwise get the tent's interior wet, you'll appreciate the elevation of a full-length pad.

Dressing for Winter

Winter clothing keeps you warm primarily by trapping air in bulky, fluffy spaces—in other words, by insulating. But if you're being active in winter and spending multiple days in the same clothes, insulation alone is not enough. That insulation has to stay dry, not just from the outside in, but from the inside out. This is where specialized outdoor clothing is literally a lifesaver. Any moisture in your clothing quickly conducts body heat straight to the atmosphere. This means that your active clothing (as compared to the super-warm down coat that you only wear in camp) must not absorb sweat; instead it must quickly transfer body moisture to your outermost layer, where it can evaporate. Specialized synthetic garments made out of variously coated, treated, woven, and plucked polyesters and nylons have made winter travel far safer than it was in the days of water-retaining wool and cotton.

Goose down is the only non-synthetic you should consider for winter camping, other than a judicious amount of wool (I think synthetics offer higher performance at less weight than wool, but some people feel a little sheepish without the old standby). Nothing is warmer than down for the weight, and feathers compress far better than do their synthetic counterparts, making down garments easier to stuff into an overfull pack.

If you're dressed adequately, cold and snow have little effect on your attitude. This camper on the Waddington Glacier, British Columbia, spits at the wind, as cheerful as he might be on a summer's day. (Photo: ©John Harlin)

Just don't break a sweat while wearing a down garment; it dries poorly and it won't keep you nearly as warm when it's wet as will good synthetics. The ideal use of down is as a bulky coat to wear in camp. By keeping your down coat handy, you can throw it on during rest stops and at lunch, thus maintaining a balanced body temperature during exercise and at rest. The best down jacket will fit over your shell clothes and will have a water-resistant/breathable shell of its own.

With today's synthetic clothing, socks are the only things you really need to change in the backcountry (dry feet are absolutely essential to preventing frostbite). Bring a fresh pair of insulating socks for each day, ideally carrying them in their own self-sealing plastic bags.

Managing the Load

It's hard enough in the summer to fit everything into your backpack. Once you add what's required for winter—additional clothes, warmer sleeping bag, more fuel and food, perhaps a second sleeping pad, a snow shovel, a roomier tent—the bulk and weight can overwhelm you. You have two options, depending on the terrain.

Sleds. The first and best option is to pull a sled instead of piling everything on your back. It's a wonder to behold how easily you can drag massive quantities of gear in a trailing sled. Polar explorers have been known to haul up to 500 pounds per person, including several months' worth of food. They weren't having fun doing it, but the point is that not even the heartiest mountain man can travel with 500 pounds on his back. The same principle holds for your winter weeklong or even weekend outing—you'll have a lot more fun pulling than humping.

This assumes that you're traveling where there's continuous snow cover and where the hills, especially the sidehills, aren't too severe. If the snow cover is patchy, you'll have to carry the sled frequently. And if the hill slopes sideways, you could spend half your day fighting the sled as it tugs you off the trail. Specialized skiers' sleds help considerably because they come equipped with runners to keep the sled on its track. You can even add optional brakes that prevent the sled from slipping backward. These sleds usually are connected to the skier via metal rods instead of ropes; these rods prevent the sled from overtaking you during downhill travel.

If you're traveling on continuous snow without too many sidehills, a sled makes hauling your bulkier and heavier snow-camping gear vastly easier; aluminum poles keep the sled spaced behind you so that it doesn't bump into you on downhill passages. (Photo: ©John Harlin)

Alas, such sleds can cost several hundred dollars and are only worthwhile if you're doing a lot of winter travel. Until then, you can do as poor mountaineers do: Drag one of those light plastic kiddy sleds, perhaps after making a few basic modifications to improve lash points. Strap in your entire pack or carry some of your gear on your back and the rest in a gunnysack or duffel bag in the sled. Just remember that if you don't have continuous snow, you will have to carry everything on your back occasionally.

Packs. A pack that's perfect for a full week's summer gear might be too small for a short weekend in winter. But don't invest in a massive pack before you know whether winter camping is really your cup of tea. Try a cheap sled if the terrain allows. Or borrow or rent an expedition-sized pack (something in the 6,000-cubic-inch range). If you have to, just buy some extra stuff sacks and creatively lash them to your summer pack. Frame packs are particularly adaptable to lashing, though they're awful for skiing (the center of gravity is too high).

On a ski tour, backpacks must be very large because there's a lot to carry if you want to stay warm in the winter. (Photo: ©John Harlin)

When you're ready to buy a pack appropriate to winter travel, make it voluminous above all (6,000-plus cubic inches) and with a suspension system that can handle bulky clothing and lots of weight. Make sure it can accommodate skis, even if you're not yet a skier—you don't want to have to reinvest once you fall in love with snow and take up this wonderful sport. Again with skiing in mind, go for an internal-frame pack because it carries the weight much better for those glorious downhill runs. These packs normally sell under the moniker of "expedition packs" because they're suitable for humping loads up Himalayan peaks. Once you own such a behemoth, you'll find yourself using it in the summer, too, whether for taking longer hikes than you previously could or for carrying more than your share of a group's load, especially if you find yourself *en famille*.

Getting Around

Under certain, limited conditions, you can tramp in hiking boots on crusty snow without sinking. Usually, however, you will break through, which quickly exhausts you and, if you're hiking a trail, earns you the enmity of every skier who follows your tracks. Snow hiking requires tools that allow you to walk on (frozen) water. This section focuses on the differences between two major types of snow travel and which is best suited to your trip; it's beyond the scope of this book to go into detail about the types of snowshoes and skis available, and how to select what's right for you (see your outdoor retailer for that).

Snowshoes. These simple, foolproof flotation devices can turn any summer hiker into a winter enthusiast. Though many skiers decry snowshoeing because it can't deliver the gliding thrills of skiing, there are occasions when even the best skier would be better off with snowshoes. Snowshoes are particularly suited to heavily wooded terrain or when you have to carry your floats over bare ground for some distance. Best of all, however, is that they allow a non-skier to get out and enjoy the snow without worrying about learning a new sport; they also don't require you to buy specialized boots.

Skis. Skiing, at its finest, is more magic than sport; it transmutes cold snow to a source of endless joy. But it takes time to learn to ski like an alchemist, and this book is no primer on the topic. Besides, merely hiking on skis is like using a sports car to pull a plow. When you're carrying a pack on your back and measuring your progress by horizontal distance covered rather than vertical distance lost, the only advantage of skis over snowshoes is that they handle sidehills more easily and they are faster on smooth or downhill passages. Nevertheless, consider skis if you find yourself inclined to use your tent as a base camp from which to stage packless raids on nearby slopes.

Special Tools for Winter

Snow shovel. A snow shovel is not only useful around camp, but it can be a lifesaver as well. In avalanche territory, you may need a shovel to dig out the unlucky. More likely, you'll use your snow shovel to dig a snow cave or other shelter, to cut blocks for building wind barriers around the tent and cooking area, for gathering snow or ice to melt into water, to use as a stove stand, and to sit on while whooping and sliding down hills. Snow shovels should be light and strong. Specialized, collapsible snow shovels are available where backcountry ski equipment is sold. You can make a snow shovel by cutting down an aluminum grain scoop, which works great. Just make sure it's strong enough to lever with.

Snowshoes are ideally suited to complex woods-walking and to those who haven't developed their skiing skills but still want to enjoy rugged winter wilderness. (Photo: ©John Harlin)

The snow shovel is an essential tool for snow campers.
(Photo: ©John Harlin)

Signal beacons. In the mountains, you need these in order to find anyone caught in an avalanche. But you also need the good sense not to need to do avalanche rescue. Take a course in winter travel so you know how to avoid avalanches—and do avalanche rescue if necessary.

Snow saws are specialized tools for hard snow. They are essential for slicing blocks while building an igloo, and convenient when building a wind barrier or snow cave in dense snow. It's hard to replicate the light-but-stiff blade of a snow saw without buying the genuine article.

Repair kit. While a repair kit might be considered optional on a mild-weather summer excursion, in the winter your life depends on your gear. If the tent or your packsack starts ripping, you'll need to repair it quickly (a stitch in time and all that), so bring at least the following: heavy-duty thread and needles, maybe an awl, some duct tape (wrap some around your ski poles to keep it handy), a spare ski pole basket, a posidrive screwdriver for repairing bindings, pliers, wire for ski or snowshoe repair, steel wool to fit in loose binding holes, and perhaps a zipper repair kit.

▲ ▲ ▲

Equipment Checklist for Snow Camping

Cooking Gear
- stove
- stove fuel (enough for melting snow for drinking water)
- several lighters
- matches
- pot(s)
- pot scrubber (optional; snow works well)
- insulated drinking mug
- bowl
- spoon
- pocket knife
- two leakproof water bottles
- insulated water-bottle container

Sleeping Gear
- tent (plus rain fly, cords, stakes that work in snow)
- ground cloth (optional)

- sleeping bag (rated to at least 10 degrees lower than what you expect to encounter)
- vapor barrier bag (optional)
- full-length insulating pad (two in supercold weather)
- pee bottle (optional)

Clothing

Everything should be quick-drying synthetic or wool especially made for rugged outdoor use—no cotton.

- two pairs liner socks (thin, quick-drying)
- one pair per day (if possible) insulating socks (thick)
- underpants (yes, synthetic)
- long underwear (bottoms and tops)
- pants
- shirt
- pile (fleece) pants
- pile vest
- pile and/or down jacket
- shell jacket (with hood) and pants (both of waterproof/breath-able fabric)
- neck gaiter or scarf
- liner gloves
- heavy gloves or mittens (plus extra pair in case you lose one)
- shell mittens
- hat
- brimmed cap for warm, sunny days
- boots (appropriate to activity; roomy enough for thick socks and toe-wiggling; waterproof)
- gaiters

Sun and Wind Protection

- goggles (for wind and snow)
- sunglasses
- sunscreen
- lip balm with sunblock

Transportation

- pack

- sled (optional)
- skis (with skins, waxes) or snowshoes
- ski poles

Navigation
- topographic map
- compass
- altimeter watch (optional but highly useful)
- Global Positioning System (GPS) (optional)

Safety Gear
- first-aid kit (check for completeness of contents)
- aspirin or substitute
- blister-prevention pads (e.g., moleskin)
- snow shovel
- snow saw
- firestarter
- whistle
- repair kit
- watch (it's important to know how much daylight remains)
- ice ax (if mountainous terrain)
- avalanche signal beacon (depending on terrain)
- cellular phone (optional)
- water purification system (optional, depending on destination and temperature)

Illumination
- headlamp
- extra batteries and bulb
- candle(s)
- lantern (optional)

Miscellaneous (all optional)
- book
- notepad or journal and pencil
- game(s)
- camera, film, extra battery
- chair conversion kit for your sleeping pad

Packing and Organizing

I rarely use a list myself. Instead, I follow a mental process that is supposed to get me to the same place. I present my system here not to replace the list (see Equipment Checklist for Snow Camping in this chapter), but to help you understand it—and to show you why even an experienced winter camper like me should use the list.

Here's my system: First, I mentally dress myself from foot to head and from base layer to outer layer (including protecting my hands and head). I pretend I'm walking out of my home directly into the worst weather I expect to encounter on my trip. Typically I lay my garments on the floor as if I'm dressing an imaginary doll.

Next I think of what I'm going to walk in (boots), what I'll keep the snow out with (gaiters), how I'll protect my eyes (goggles, sunglasses) and my skin (sunscreen), what I'll sleep in (sleeping bag), what I'll sleep on (pad), what my home will be (tent), how I'll cook and eat my food (stove, stove stand, pot, cup, bowl, spoon), how I'll light my fire (lighter, matches), what I'll eat (food—its own elaborate process, breakfast to dinner), how I'm going to see while cooking (headlamp, candle, maybe a lantern), and how I'll carry this massive pile of stuff (backpack, sled).

Then comes my transportation method (skis or snowshoes, ski poles, skins or waxes for skis). I think of where I'm going and how I'm going to find my way (map, compass, maybe a GPS) and what I might encounter (avalanche signal beacon, snow shovel). Then I think of what might happen in an emergency (first-aid kit, maybe a cellular phone, firestarter, whistle, extra matches).

Finally, I'll think of optional items to keep me entertained during a long winter night (book, notepad or journal, micro chess set).

As an exercise, I wrote the above process completely out of my head. But now I'm in my usual quandary before jumping into the car: What did I forget? So I check my list (see Equipment Checklist for Snow Camping) and see that I forgot two essentials: a water bottle and fuel for my stove. I also forgot some things I could have made do without, like extra batteries, pot grippers, camera, and film. All in all, my system worked pretty well, but if I had really headed down the trail without a water bottle or stove fuel, I'd have to turn back, maybe after spending a very hungry and cold night. My partners would be upset because I probably spoiled the whole trip. So you see the value of a list, no matter how well you understand winter camping.

Special Considerations for Winter Camping

Winter is a serious affair. Wild animals are starving and freezing in just the conditions where we snow campers are frolicking. Remove a small number of our technological aids, and humans are far less prepared for the cold than are the beasts. When you're out there having a good time, remember that a mistake (getting lost, damaging a stove, losing a sleeping bag or tent, breaking a bone, falling into a stream) can turn your world upside down. So can a rapid change in weather. Suddenly you'll be relying on skills you may not have yet developed. Use your head, and you'll probably be okay. Lose it, and you'll freeze.

Survival considerations. If you think that a storm is rolling in, try to get out before it hits. If you can't, batten down the hatches and prepare to sleep it out. Don't try to move during bad weather unless you're supremely skilled at foul-weather navigation. Make sure that your tent is pitched well, as out of the wind as you can get it (or protected by a wind wall), and away from avalanche run-outs (the vast majority of naturally triggered avalanches slide during storms). Not even the side of the valley opposite an avalanche path is safe, because a big one can sweep across the valley and travel uphill a way.

While the snow is falling, make sure that it doesn't build up too heavily on or against the tent. When thwacking the walls from the inside fails to do the trick, get out there and shovel it away from the walls (being very careful not to cut the tent or a guy line). Gradually collapsing walls cut off air circulation. Eventually the camel's-backbreaking flake will land, buckling the tent. You may need to get out several times during the night to ensure your peace of mind.

The storm may last for days. If it does, you have no option but to wait it out. Don't think of missed deadlines back home, or even of worried loved ones or search parties. Conserve food and fuel if you're running low, maintain your cool, and patiently ride it out. The storm will end eventually, and you'll need your wits, energy, and stove fuel to find your way home again. Just be sure that nothing vital (skis, snowshoes, pack) is buried where you can't uncover it when the time comes to get the heck out of there.

Sudden plunging temperatures are another matter; it might just stay there for a while. If the mercury plummets below where you feel psychologically or physically comfortable, head for home, but do it as wisely as possible. A misstep now and you could be in trouble. Chances are that your clothing and sleeping bag will get you through a few nights even if you have to shiver. Travel by day, as efficiently as you can. Don't push too hard—take brief rest breaks when you need them. But keep moving until early dusk, then make camp before it gets dark.

Stay bundled and don't risk anything. If you're getting chilled, never take off your mittens no matter how awkward a process is. Never grow blasé about such things as wearing hats and hoods, or finding snow creeping into your boots or down your neck. Force yourself to do the smart thing, even if—especially if—your mind is growing numb and weary. You may have to think outside of yourself to do the right thing, but whatever it takes, stay in control.

Because you'll likely be with someone else, monitor each other. Sometimes it's easier to see that your partner is making cold-induced mistakes than it is to catch them in yourself. Once you see it in your partner, you might recognize it in yourself. Often these mistakes come from a strange kind of laziness. If you don't let your partner or yourself get away with anything, you'll eventually make it back to the car and, in due time, a long, hot bath.

Cold injuries. Your two main concerns in winter are both cold-related. Hypothermia is when your core body temperature drops, which can happen without any body parts freezing. Frostbite is when body parts freeze, which can happen without a drop in core body temperature. All winter campers with a sense of responsibility for themselves and their companions should consult a wilderness first-aid/medicine primer to learn more about these winter maladies.

Winter living. There's something terribly, wonderfully elemental about winter. You can observe it while staring out the window across a snowy landscape. Venture out for a day of snowshoeing or skiing, and winter starts to slip under your skin. But it takes living with winter, not

watching it, for its essence to penetrate your core. That elemental pen-
etration isn't always what you want to feel, certainly not if what's scratch-
ing at your bones is an unshakable chill. Winter is a serious time.

But if you're prepared to meet the season on your terms, you'll travel
a magical trail ever deeper into the heart of snow season. Old Man Winter may be a stern taskmaster, but his soul reveals truth and beauty not
found in the lusher seasons. Travel wisely, and perhaps you'll become fast
friends.

SETTING UP CAMP

Choosing a Winter Campsite

On the whole, choosing a winter camp and choosing a summer camp
are similar, except that in winter such elements as wind and sun take on
greater significance. Patches of bare ground in the forest duff, or ridges
that have been baked by the sun, often make for warmer and cozier
camping than you'll find on snow. (Beware, however: It might have
been recurring wind that carried away the snow.) Still, consider avoiding those bare patches. One of the great beauties of snow camping is
that you have almost zero environmental impact. But if you hang out
on a small patch of dry ground, especially in your big, clunky mountain
boots, you can cause a huge amount of damage to sensitive alpine environments. Unless the snow-free patch is bare mineral soil, the local
flora and fauna would thank you to stick to thick snow. Camping on
thin snow can also be harmful because compacting the snow delays its
melting, and in alpine zones with a short growing season, this can make
a big difference to the plants below.

Also on an environment-friendly note, avoid camping where there
are a lot of animal signs. The critters have a tough enough time in winter;
try to leave them some peace in their favorite hangout or feeding places.

Wind. Summer wind flaps your tent walls and keeps the bugs
away; winter wind is a bit more troublesome. It carries off whatever
envelope of heat your tent might otherwise have developed; it can make
cooking outside a misery if not impossible; and it can drift snow against
your tent, potentially even crushing it. A summer-weight tent used in
winter can be flattened by the wind itself, never mind the snow it carries.

A well-placed, completely secured tent makes a perfect base camp for day skiing. (Photo: ©John Harlin)

If it's blowing when you pitch your tent, you have a pretty good idea of what you might be in for—expect more of the same, if not harder.

But if you pitch your tent when things are calm, take a look at the snow's surface. Is it obviously wind-sculpted? Does that flat spot you picked have a peculiar look to it, like it's been scoured into the slope? Is your would-be campsite firm and crusty when nearby snow is soft and fluffy? These could be indications that you've found a mini (or maxi) wind funnel, which is not where you want to camp. Sometimes a few feet can make an enormous difference in wind strength. Look for clues before you commit yourself for the night.

Cold pockets. Valley floors are often the chilliest places to camp because cold air settles in from all sides. If you remember conditions in fall meadows, you'll recall that low spots typically frost the deepest and stay frosty longest. The same is true on a larger scale in winter. You'll probably be warmest camping on the hill somewhat above the valley bottom.

Sun. Try to pick a site that will face the earliest morning sun. There's no describing the morale boost of having the first rays of the day warm your tent. Contrast that with observing the sun on the opposite side of the valley while you're watching your breath freeze in the crunchy air; where would you rather awaken?

Avalanche. Wind, frost pockets, and orientation to the sun pale into insignificance compared with avalanche safety. In the mountains, avalanches are the great insidious monsters lurking beneath the calm white seas. By day you'll travel through various situations where sliding snow is more and less a concern. When you set up camp, you're likely to spend 15 or more hours, perhaps even a few days if a storm materializes, in exactly the same spot. Be absolutely certain that you're well out of any danger zones.

Think less about the slope you're on (after all, you're unlikely to set up camp on the 25- to 45-degree slope that's most likely to avalanche) and think much more about the slope above you, both on your side of the valley and the opposite side. Look for clues that avalanches have visited your site. Is there a swath cut out of the trees? Are there broken limbs lying about, or damaged trunks? Most obvious is a debris pile of snow below. But also look above, way above. Any gullies leading your way? Snow collection zones in the craggy heights? Don't even think about spending the night where there are any signs that there ever was an avalanche, or where there seems to be the potential for one. Even if it hasn't snowed for weeks, the big storm could roll in tonight, loading every treacherous slope above your camp. Something else to think about, even if your campsite is safe: Will you be trapped tomorrow? Avoid camping between danger zones that would put you at risk on your way out.

Arrival in Camp

Divvy up your human resources. Assign a person or two to the task of setting up the tent(s) while the other(s) gather ice, water, and firewood if necessary, and start setting up the camp kitchen. If you have two or more stoves, a person or two can be assigned to brewing drinks and refilling water bottles while the other(s) prepare dinner. These chores can be rotated or shared depending on your preferences or talents.

Once you've picked a nice safe spot to camp, pack the snow where you'll be walking and pitching the tent. If you set the tent straight on

Your tent's door is its window on the world, so if you want to catch the sunrise, point it east. Keep wind direction in mind. In the winter the door should face leeward so snow or rain doesn't blow in, while in bug country in the summer it should face into the breeze to help keep the beasties outside. (Photo: ©John Harlin)

unconsolidated snow, you'll battle unbelievable lumpiness. So spend a few minutes, even a half hour, using your skis or snowshoes to thoroughly pack down the tent site, the region around the tent, and the cooking site. This is some of the most valuable time you'll spend. Then wait a half hour, if possible, before setting up the tent to allow the snow to firm up by recrystallizing.

Dressing for Camp Comfort

If you arrive in camp dry or with just a little sweat in your clothes, both of which are normal in snow travel, then you'll cool gradually while making camp and as the evening progresses. Take off your shell jacket early and put on a warm and cozy down jacket or a fleece jacket. Put your shell back on if you need the weather protection or if it's slightly damp and you need your body heat to drive the moisture from the jacket.

If you're soaked from sweat, change into something dry. You'll get chilled quickly if you stand around waiting for your clothes to dry on your body. Don't just put on thick insulating layers, because your body heat will drive the moisture from your wet layers outward and humidify your fresh insulation. But because the quickest way to dry synthetic clothing in the winter is by wearing it, once you've removed your wet garments you'll have to find another way to dry them (try hanging them out to freeze and sublimate). Let this be a lesson to slow down or wear less clothing before arriving in camp next time, giving your clothing a chance to dry out before you stop for the day.

Rehydrate

Chances are very good that you didn't drink as much as you should have during the course of the day. One reason is that when it's cold out, most of us have a hard time forcing ourselves to drink as much as our bodies need. The other reason is that we rarely have any idea that we're perspiring as much as we really are. In the dry cold of winter, our sweat tends to evaporate quickly through our synthetic clothing and breathable shell, which means we never feel it wet against our skin. But we're still losing lots of moisture. So one of the first things you should do in camp is to finish drinking whatever water is left in your bottle or thermos, then take out the stove and melt some more water and drink this too. You can wait until the tent is set up to fire up the stove, but a good time to begin melting water might be while you're waiting for the snow to settle where you've tamped it down for your tent site.

Before setting up the tent, stomp out a firm, flat platform using your skis or snowshoes and wait a half hour for the snow to set up before erecting the tent. (Photo: ©John Harlin)

Pitching Your Tent

If you're camping in a group with two or more tents, place the tents so that the doors are within arm's reach of each other. This allows communal cooking, sharing of food and drink, and storytelling to proceed even if you're not in the mood to crawl out of your bag.

Even if your tent is freestanding, securing the guy lines is a wise move in case the wind picks up or heavy snow falls. Easiest is to use skis, poles, or snowshoes as anchor points. If these are unavailable, you can tie off your tent stake in the middle (or use a stick if you can find one longer than your stake, or even use a buried stuff sack or rock), bury it in the snow, and tamp it hard. Or pack down the snow until it's firm, wait for it to consolidate, then cut a bollard (a pear-shaped groove with the skinny end pointed toward the tent) and loop some webbing around it. When

Strong winds buffet the tents at this camp at the base of Longs Peak in Colorado. Angling the tent doors to face one another would have allowed cooked food and hot drinks to be handed back and forth between the tents. (Photo: ©John Harlin)

Anchor guy lines with skis or snowshoes when possible. (Photo: ©John Harlin)

Anchors

Snow anchors can include (a) buried objects such as tent stakes, sticks, rocks, or stuff sacks full of rocks or other objects, (b) bollards, and (c) skis. Tension knots (tautline or rolling hitches) are used so that guy line tension can be adjusted. (See illustration in chapter 1.)

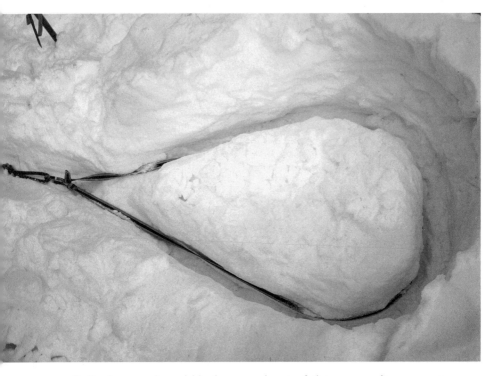

Bollards, pear-shaped blocks carved out of the surrounding snow, can sometimes be useful for tying off tent guy lines in high winds. (Photo: ©John Harlin)

it's cut to a size appropriate to the snow conditions, a bollard can withstand large pulling forces. But standard tent guy lines are generally too short, thin, and round to tie off bollards with.

Another reason to keep the guy lines taut is to keep the tent walls widely spaced. If you develop condensation inside the tent, each time you brush its walls you could find a little snowstorm settling on your sleeping bag. Best not to have to touch the walls. To minimize condensation, avoid cooking inside the tent (discussed further in The Camp Kitchen section later in this chapter) and keep as much air flow going as you find acceptable. The more air flow, the colder it will be in your tent, so this is definitely a trade-off situation. Monitor how your tent is breathing and how warm you need it to be inside, and adjust the vents accordingly.

Coping with heavy snow or wind. Snow is something you expect while snow camping, and it's rarely a problem. But occasionally it comes a little too fast and furious, or is particularly heavy. In mild form, this could push the rain fly of your tent against the inner tent wall, which can lead to condensation, drip-through, or even loss of air exchange. In a more extreme form, the tent walls collapse inward; if the tent poles snap, you're in trouble.

Under such a snowstorm, you have to keep *thwap-thwapping* the tent walls every so often to keep the snow from accumulating on them. Snow slides down and builds up on the sides of the tent, gradually compressing the lower reaches ever inward. Periodically dig this snow away from the tent. How often this cycle happens simply depends on the extent of the snowfall. If it's a big dump, you have to keep up with it, period, maybe even digging out several times a night. Far more likely is that you'll just *thwap* the tent walls whenever you wake up during the night. It's all part of the fun of being outdoors in winter. You're in the real world now.

These crushed tents, abandoned just before a storm struck, are vivid examples of why snow campers have to shovel away accumulating snow. (Photo: ©John Harlin)

This dome tent at 17,000 feet on Mount Huascaran in Peru is deformed by severe winds that sprang up in the middle of the night. If you're in a potentially windy environment, completely stake out all of the guy lines before going to bed so you won't have to attempt the process in a blizzard at night. (Photo: ©John Harlin)

Many people build snow walls on the windward side of the tent to deflect the breezes. These can be mixed blessings, however, because during a storm the snow can drift in behind the wall, radically increasing the accumulation around your tent. If you build a snow wall, leave plenty of room to maneuver with your snow shovel between the tent and the wall. Ideal is to build the wall 6 feet away from your tent. This way, most of the drift should settle before it reaches your sleeping quarters. I've also heard that building two walls spaced 6 feet apart is best—that way most of the snow collects between the two walls and none reaches your tent. Makes good sense to me, but I've yet to try it.

Snow walls help keep the wind from buffeting a tent, but if they're placed too close, snow drifting behind the wall can bury the tent. Note how the skis here are positioned vertically so they won't be buried by falling or drifting snow. (Photo: ©John Harlin)

How to Build Snow Wall

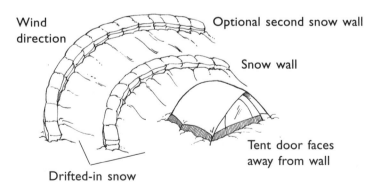

Build one snow wall about 6 feet from your tent so that snow fills in behind the wall rather than on your tent. The second snow wall is optional.

Tenting in shelters. Along certain popular routes, such as the Appalachian Trail, you'll find a network of roofed three-sided shelters. In winter, you can set up your tent inside the shelter for more protection and warmth. The advantage is that you can easily get by with a three-season tent because you'll not be facing extreme wind or snow loads. The disadvantage is that these shelters are often dank and dark, and all the more so in winter. But with a good lantern, the place perks up; it's certainly roomier than just hanging out inside a tent.

Snow Shelters

For the ultimate snow experience, try camping *in* it rather than on it. Snow shelters are warmer than tents, and you don't have to carry them on your back. But they do take time to build. I'm not fond of them for this reason, and because living in a snow shelter, ironically, isolates you from the environment more than does living in a tent. A blizzard might be raging out there, but within the muffled recesses of your snow cave, you'd think all was peaceful. The thermometer might be shattering from the chill, but in your snow cave you are warm and comfortable. Or, the sun might rise in a spectacular display; you, in your cave, think it's the middle of the night. I prefer to be out there in it—well, not exactly bivouacking, but at least not hidden behind thick, windowless walls. Also, I prefer spending my time cruising, eating, and watching rather than digging and carving tunnels in snow.

But there are innumerable situations where snow shelters are the ticket: for a serious base camp, when you need more shelter than your tent can provide, if you lost your tent (say, it broke in a storm), if you don't own a four-season tent, when the weather is truly cold or foul—or if you just plain disagree with me on one or all of my objections!

Snow caves. To build a snow cave, you'll need a bank of snow deep enough to tunnel into, with at least 1 foot of snow to spare around the chamber walls. This translates to at least a 6-foot snow depth (preferably much more) filling a space at least 6 feet wide by 8 feet long. You're much better off, however, with greater depth and area in which to work. Such depths are typically found in accumulation zones on the lee sides of ridges. The steeper the face of this snowdrift, the better.

The basic principle is that you want an upwardly sloping tunnel leading to a sleeping chamber. The sleeping chamber can be carved into

Construction of a snow cave requires a steep embankment filled with plenty of snow. The walls and ceiling must be 1 foot thick, and the entrance hole should rise toward the interior so that cold air drains down and out. (Photo: ©John Harlin)

whatever shape you like, but at a minimum it should have one or two sleeping platforms and a trench that collects the cold air. This cold air should be allowed to drain down the sloping tunnel entrance. You'll want at least 1 foot of snow thickness over the roof and around the walls. And you'll want an air hole punched through the roof.

First carve a notch into the drift so that you have a vertical area to start your tunnel in. It's easiest to dig the entrance tunnel at a comfortable size (say, a stooped working height) and fill it back in with blocks of snow. Use your snow shovel or, if you forgot it, carve with pots, snowshoes, ice axes, or mittened hands. Dress lightly and wear waterproof/breathable clothing. This is sweaty work, and wet, too, because snow will likely melt against, maybe even in, your steaming clothing. Don't work so hard that you saturate your garments. It's best to have one person carving and another stationed at the entryway to shovel the snow away. If you're short on space for tunneling, build a tunnel with the carvings, or even heap them on the outside of the cave to supplement its depth.

Carve the entryway angling slightly uphill (make it several feet long if you have the room), then begin your living quarters. Give yourself as much space as the drift and your time allow. If possible, you should be able to stand up in the cold-air sink and sit up comfortably on the sleeping platforms. Make it wide enough that you don't touch the walls while sleeping. Condensation could form on the snow, especially while you're cooking, and you don't want it in contact with your bag (bivy sacks are great for keeping your sleeping bag dry). A domed ceiling is the strongest shape and it also reduces the likelihood of water drippage if the snow is wet. Given enough time and space, you can carve multiple chambers, alcoves, shelves, tables, anything your imagination desires.

Finally, don't forget to punch that ventilation hole in the ceiling. An arm's thickness is good, even a wiggled ski pole thickness will do. You can leave the ski pole in the hole to keep it open if snow drifts over. Shrink the size of the entryway by partially blocking it with snow or backpacks. And be sure to keep a snow shovel inside in case the entry drifts over (remember, you've probably built this thing in an accumulation zone, so you can expect more of the same if there's any wind or snowfall).

Snow trenches. A snow trench is also known as a "snow grave." If you don't have the time or the snow supply to build a full cave, but you need a shelter from the wind, you can dig a simple trench wide enough to

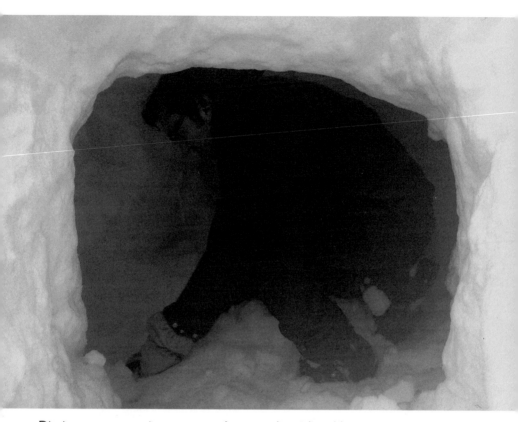

Digging snow caves is sweaty work, even when it's cold out; wear water-proof shell clothing and not too much insulation so you don't get wet from the inside out. (Photo: ©John Harlin)

sit in, long enough for two people to face each other, and deep enough to keep you out of the wind. You should be able to do this in 10 minutes or so, depending on how hard the snow is. To make a roof, you need ski poles, skis, and a bivy sack. Place your ski poles across the completed trench; insert your skis into the bivy sack (or wrap your rain fly around the skis); and lay the skis/bivy sack combo onto the poles as a roof.

This process is so quick that you could use it to escape the wind, if necessary, during a lunch break. In an emergency you could sleep in such a trench. Be sure to dig a deeper section where the cold air can sink. And don't build the trench too wide or you'll have trouble supporting the roof, especially if there's heavy snowfall.

If there's a firm layer of snow from which you can cut blocks, try slicing panels that you can lean against each other A-frame-style above the trench, thus creating a strong roof that doesn't require skis and will better keep out snow during a prolonged stay in your trench. Be sure to fill in your trench when you're done with it, so later travelers don't unwittingly become entombed.

Quin-zhees. If the snow is shallow, don't despair; just pile it up until you have what you need! To make this Athapaskan snow shelter, first mark out a circle 7 or 8 feet in diameter and heap snow on it until it's as deep as you need—remember that you'll want 1-foot-thick walls and ceiling. Once the snow is piled 6 or 7 feet high, let it sit for an hour so that it can settle and recrystallize into a consolidated mass. Then go in and carve out your shelter, just as you would a snow cave. Remember to punch an air hole in the ceiling. And, just as in a snow cave, try to have a rising entrance and a trench below the sleeping platform for cold air to settle into.

Making a Quin-zhee

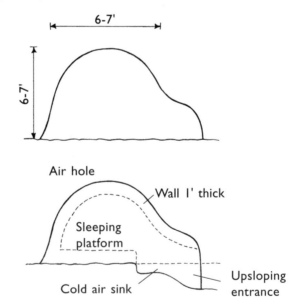

a. Start with flat ground. Pile up snow and then wait 1 hour for snow to set.
b. Dig out quin-zhee.

Don't get caught out overnight without adequate shelter. There isn't even enough snow here to dig a snow cave—these "campers" have dug down to bare ice. An option would have been to pile snow into a big mound, let it solidfy, and then carve out a quin-zhee. (Photo: ©John Harlin)

Igloos. These are the most famous, and the most complex, of snow shelters. They are particularly suited to wide-open environments where the snow is flat and firm. The idea is to carve rectangular blocks out of this firm snow and spiral them around and over what will become the interior space. You'll need a snow saw to carve the shaped blocks that are ideally suited to building an igloo. Igloo construction is a specialized technique beyond the scope of this book. Once you've spent a lot of time outdoors in winter, you might devote a few idle hours to having fun with such a project.

Natural shelters. It is rare that you'd choose a natural shelter instead of a tent or something you carve out of the snow yourself. But in case of emergency, you can try to search out some natural shelter. In the miraculous event that a cave is nearby, take it if it's not occupied by an ursine or feline character.

More likely you'll find shelter among the trees. Look for a deep tree well. Often snow cascades down a tree's branches, leaving a depression around the trunk itself; this tree well can offer protection from wind and falling snow. Dense branches or brush thickets also can offer shelter. Likely you'll need to crawl into position; just be careful not to shake loose all the accumulated snow above as you slither among the branches. If you're on a glacier, you can sometimes find a shallow crevasse to scramble into for protection against the wind.

THE CAMP KITCHEN

Once you reach camp, change into warm and/or dry clothes, rehydrate, and erect the tent(s), you'll be faced with a grand dilemma: whether to dine in or out. Dining out means setting up a kitchen in the snow. Weather permitting, you'll be under the stars experiencing more of the environment that drew you away from the comforts of home. If you're sharing your adventure with a larger group that occupies multiple tents, this will likely be your preferred choice.

If it's just you and your mate in one tent, or if the weather is inclement, you'll be awfully tempted to dine in. You'll probably crawl into your warm bags and cook your meal through the tent door or in the tent vestibule. Even if you occupy multiple tents, you can still live communally by pitching tents with the doors an arm's reach apart.

Here is an outdoor dining setup that I've never tried but that sounds marvelous. Campers dig a large dish out of the snow, 6 to 8 feet across and a couple of feet deep. Snow that is shoveled out is piled around the perimeter, or upwind if breezes are an issue. Seats can be cut or punched in the dish's walls. In the center of the circle, a fire is built. The snow walls reflect the fire's light and heat; the chairs sit everyone comfortably facing each other so that fire-enhanced conversations flow freely.

My personal snow-camping experiences have leaned toward single-tent parties in locations or situations where fires were impossible or inappropriate; consequently I've had too much tent-bound living. But this communal cook pit sounds so appealing that I can't wait to try it, even without a fire.

Winter Stove Considerations

Be sure to understand your stove intimately, because you'll use it a lot. Keep your stove well maintained. Here are a few points that are particularly salient to cold-weather stove use.

White gas is by far the most efficient fuel, and stoves that use it are the standard for winter use, especially because often it's necessary to melt snow or ice for all drinking and cooking needs. However, the priming process of a white gas stove can create flare-ups that are extremely difficult to control.

The only advantage of blended-fuel cartridge stoves or isobutane stoves is that they are safer to light and to use inside the tent. You should in fact never cook inside, but foul weather and sheer convenience often turn otherwise rational campers into rule-breakers. But never, ever light a stove inside the tent. If exceptionally bad weather forces you to do it anyway, you'll want a canister stove. For this reason, inclement-weather mountaineers sometimes use these stoves despite their relative inefficiency.

Be careful that your hot stove doesn't melt its way into the snow. You can use a piece of closed-cell foam pad wrapped in duct tape, an old license plate, a commercial stove base, or even a metal snow shovel to create a stove base.

Wood Fires

You're usually much better off with an efficient camp stove, but in most environments a wood fire is an emergency backup in case your stove fails. Bring firestarter or be otherwise proficient at finding burnable wood and lighting it. These days, wood fires are deservedly maligned. This doesn't mean that you can't make and enjoy them; it just means you should be environmentally sensitive about the process, paying careful attention to the fire's consequences. On snowy ground, these consequences mimic those of summer, with some slight variations.

For example, in summer wood is typically gathered in the vicinity of popular campgrounds. In winter, anything on the ground is buried under snow. This means you'll need to rip dead branches off of standing trees or saw down dead trees. If you're in a little-visited area, neither of these is a problem. But in a popular area, the trees rapidly get stripped and cut. Do you want to contribute to this phenomenon? Best is to try to gather wood from as far afield as possible so as to spread the impact.

Also consider the fact that your coals will drop to the ground when the snow melts. Don't let this happen on a popular summer spot like a trail or campground. Best is to burn your wood to ash. Next best is to

Use some sort of base for your stove so it doesn't disappear in the snow. (Photo: ©Dorcas Miller)

gather up your coals and scatter them across the landscape. Alas, the morning after the fire, you might find the coals solidly encased in refrozen ice.

Speaking of melting, that's what will happen under your fire. Pack the snow down hard before building the fire. You can insulate under the fire with rotten logs, branches, or wet leaves, if you can find these. Alas, these can char and become unsightly, maybe smoky. Best is to bring a baking sheet, thick aluminum foil, or some other unburnable material to construct your fire upon. Most important is not to melt all the way through a thin snow cover until the fire burns the plants and soil underneath. You might think you're building an enviro-friendly on-snow fire, only to end up blighting an otherwise pristine meadow below.

Tricks for Snow Dining

If you're trying to keep a pot warm without leaving it on the stove, don't set it directly on the snow, which acts as a conductor of heat. Wind, too, sucks heat from the pot, and the ambient air could be colder than the snow itself (though less conductive). Try carving or punching a hole in the snow big enough for your pot. Put something insulative on the floor to set the pot on, and make sure that there is dead air space around the pot. You can cover the hole if possible, but don't use clothing or a sleeping bag because steam rising from the pot will collect in the garment.

The threads on the lip of water bottles freeze up quickly and need to be banged free. I often fill my canteen with hot water and an herbal tea bag before hitting the trail; the warmth and flavor make me more inclined to drink. In serious cold, wear the bottle on a cord inside your jacket; just be sure the seal is completely trustworthy.

Getting Drinking Water

Obtaining water in the winter often isn't a simple affair. Melting snow is a common solution, but you're better off if you can find liquid water or ice. An enormous volume of dry snow is required to make a potful of water because there's so much air trapped therein (wet snow, on the other hand, can be almost pure water). Ice is far more efficient to melt, and it stacks neatly next to your cooking area. It's worth the trouble to track down some ice or to slice up a bunch of crusty snow that has thawed and refrozen a few times on its way to becoming ice. Next to the stove, make a big pile of the densest stuff you can find. If you have to melt snow, try to prime the pot with a cup or two of liquid water so the pot doesn't scorch. If the snow is dry, it quickly absorbs the free water, so add snow slowly at first. Once you have a few inches of water in the pot, you can start packing the snow in. Again, wet snow or ice is easier.

Whenever you bring water from its crystalline (frozen) to its liquid state, you have to add 80 calories of heat per gram. That's a lot of stove gas—and time to burn it. You're much better off starting with liquid water. Find a flowing stream or dig down to the lake or stream ice and chop a hole. Just be careful that you don't break through the ice yourself.

Contrasting Snowmelt

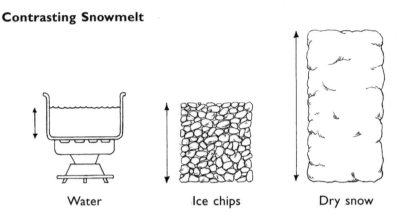

Water   Ice chips   Dry snow

It's much more efficient to melt ice than snow for drinking water.

If you're using stream or lake water, purify it to remove water-borne pathogens like *Giardia lamblia*. (See chapter 1.) Don't rely on a filter, because it will likely freeze up. If I'm melting snow for drinking water, I often won't bother bringing it to a boil—unless I don't like the looks of the tiny snow worms that often swim around in my drink. Ice sometimes holds specks of dirt and debris that is probably safe but doesn't always look pretty; boil it if you're nervous about such things.

SANITATION

Winter peeing has its special considerations. The first is the inconvenience of exposing oneself to the elements after fumbling with multiple layers of clothing. The other is the unsightly residue, which I think of as a biodegradable form of litter—sure, it breaks down and doesn't hurt the environment, but who wants to look at it in the meantime? Considerate folks take care of business next to a tree, into a bush, or anyplace where the yellow stain doesn't mar the view. When peeing out in the open, simply keep the urine flowing down a tight hole that melts in the snow. In fluffy powder, I'll usually punch a hole with my ski pole and use that to hide my mess.

Around camp, take the added precaution of not relieving yourself where you'll be gathering snow to melt for drinking water. If your tent has two doors and the wind isn't a problem, you can designate one door

serious problem. Once damp or wet, they can
f ice at night. Drying them is a difficult, time-
can hold them over a camp stove, but keep them
hey never experience any real heat (it's way too
at bonds the sole or rand to the leather; once the
s can quickly delaminate). Even if you handhold
ove, steam will still pour out of them as if from a fog
ing can make a big difference to your comfort the

ture drops well below freezing at night, do what it
boots from turning into ice blocks. At a minimum,
and bring them inside the tent, perhaps keeping them
I often take the next step, putting them in plastic bags
em into my sleeping bag at night. I bought an extra-long
ommodate boots at the bottom. I also sometimes sleep
ind my bended knees. This might be more than you find
ecessary, but it's an option to consider. It makes them easier
the morning, and my warm feet thank me during those
s of the day.

sing a sled and can handle the extra weight, consider bringing
of those mattress-chair conversion kits, or even a separate roll-
chair. These can make long hours of hanging out a lot more
table, especially if your back is getting on in years.

SHUTTING DOWN FOR THE DAY

ing Activities

erything goes according to schedule and you're ready to get a long
ht's sleep after each hard-earned day, you might consider books, games,
d other luxuries to be so much dead weight. But remember that winter
the season of storms, and many is the camper who, tentbound for the
hird day in a row, has taken to memorizing the labels on his garments
and the ingredients of his freeze-dried food. This, after ripping his
partner's book in half so that it can be shared. Games are not a laughing
matter to winter campers.

for peeing out of. If the wind isn't cooperative, you can use a pee bottle. Mark it with a skull and crossbones and be sure not to reach for the wrong bottle in the dark. Obviously, men have an easier time with such bottles. Some women use a cook pot. There are also devices made that discreetly funnel a woman's urine through a tube and into a bottle.

Far more difficult is solid waste. You'll be doing heavy battle with your conscience because it's no fun to do the right thing. What you should do is pack it out. After all, your deposit stays there all winter and then drops to the ground in the spring. In many national parks and popular federally managed wild areas (especially on certain snowy Northwest mountains in the summer), the required method is to "blue bag" it. The managing agency usually dispenses the "blue bags" and collects them, too.

In the absence of such an official system, improvise. Bring two plastic bags per expected need, one relatively thin and one sturdier; one or both bags should be an opaque color. Defecate directly onto the snow. Slip your hand into the thinner plastic bag and collect the material with it, including your used toilet paper. This becomes a bagful of doo-doo without in any way contaminating your hand. Use a wire-twist to seal this bag, then place it in the sturdier opaque bag, and wire-twist this one shut as well. You've double-bagged it and can now carry it out with a clean conscience. The opaque colored bag hides the contents (hence "blue bag"). Because temperatures are usually low in the winter, your bags may very well freeze solid and be surprisingly tolerable to pack out.

Such a system is the right thing to do in areas that are popular in the winter or that are popular immediately after spring melt-off. It's also the right thing to do if said melt-off could carry your waste into a nearby water source.

If you've taken advantage of winter's snow to explore off-trail where no one visits in the spring, and if you're more than 200 feet from the nearest stream, you can leave your dung in the snow. Choose your site with spring in mind, thinking about where your deposit will reach terra firma. In the middle of a dense thicket is a good spot. Carry a lighter in your toilet paper bag so you can burn your used toilet paper. Or gather it and carry it out.

Winter Hygiene

Keeping clean in winter is usually much easier than in summer. For one, there's less dirt about. Two, germs don't spread well in the cold. Three, there's always snow available to scrub yourself with (even your privates). In fact, if the sun breaks out, a quick snow bath is surprisingly easy—and remarkably tolerable, sometimes pleasant. You can wipe dishes with snow before, maybe even instead of, melting water to do the job. Still, it's a good idea to boil bowls, cups, and utensils periodically, especially if you're with a group. Keep your scrub-snow and scrub-water 100 feet away from the cooking and living areas. It's awfully easy to get casual about such things and soon be faced with a visual mess of discolored snow and food refuse.

CAMP COMFORTS

If your friends think that your sudden interest in snow camping reflects otherwise hidden masochistic tendencies, they're only partially right. Although snow campers don't mind testing themselves a little, the fact is we'll do what it takes to be comfortable—we usually have totally congenial experiences. It's just a bit more of a hassle than your friends are used to.

Drying Your Gear

The number-one rule, for safety as well as for personal comfort, is to keep your gear dry. Even if water doesn't penetrate from the outside, your body generates it from the inside. This perspiration, both sensible and insensible, passes through your clothing and sleeping bag, and gradually collects there. Body heat is pretty good at pushing this moisture out through your many layers of clothing. But if your garb is thick enough or contains a barrier to rapid moisture movement, sometimes that moisture starts freezing, or at least condensing, in the outer layers. Dry these whenever you get the chance. Sometimes you can just hang them outside, even in the bitter cold, and let them sublimate, especially when the sun is out. You can also wear them closer to your skin periodically, thus using body heat to drive the moisture out.

Socks are the most important item of clothing and the most likely to get wet, from the outside or inside. Have a fresh pair for each day. When this isn't practical, dry them however you can. Pin yesterday's pair to the back of your pack while you're moving. Hang them on a clothesline

It is very important to dry all [c]
chance you get. You'll stay warme[r]
weather blows in. (Photo: ©John [

214   ▼

Boots pose the most [
freeze to a solid chunk o[
consuming process. You [
far enough away that t[
easy to heat the glue t[
glue warms, the boo[t
them high over the st[
machine. Partial dry[
next day.

If the tempera[
takes to keep you[
dust off the snow[
in a plastic bag.[
and bringing th[
bag just to acc[
with them be[
tolerable or n[
to put on in[
coldest hou[

inside the tent at night. Wear them [
the sack. Wear them in your sleeping [
get the bag wet—and if you can still stay[
not soaked, leave them loose in your sle[
fact, drying damp gear by sleeping with it[
only do this if your bag is plenty insulative[
despite the damp clothing inside. If you will ge[
to the edge and any extra dampness in your bag[
effect on a future night's sleep, don't risk it. Be[
you're warm and moving than chilled while you're [

You can also build a fire and wear the clothing whi[
the flames. But drying anything by a fire is a risky pro[
synthetic clothes won't go up in a ball of flames, but the[
spark can burn a hole in your expensive outdoor cloth[
over a flame—wood fire or stove—easily melt. Even if [
melt early, you'll be left with a blister-causing ridge line o[
So be extremely careful if you use an open flame to dry anythi[
risk anything you're not willing to melt a hole into.

Chairs

If you're [
along on[
up cam[
comfor[

Eve[
If e[
nig[
an[
is[
t[

Securing Camp

In the winter, you'll always be going to bed long after the stars are out. If you've done your cooking outdoors, you'll be eager to crawl into your warm sack as soon as possible. But don't forget one absolutely essential chore: Gather up everything outside and deal with it as if you were expecting the greatest blizzard of the winter to roll in. Even if you only get a few inches of snow—or if it doesn't snow at all, but the wind scatters a few drifts here and there—uncollected gear can vanish. So don't get lazy, no matter how bright the stars are.

Plunge your skis or snowshoes vertically into the snow. Loop your ski pole straps over your skis so they don't blow over. Put everything in storage bags and bring them into the tent if there's room, or place them under the rain fly or inside your vertically standing pack. Nothing should be left loose in the snow.

If you plan to heat up water in the morning while luxuriating in the warmth of your bag, pile up a mass of ice chips or crusty snow next to the vestibule the night before. Put the stove and cook pot there too.

Most important, however, is to make yourself a hot water bottle or two so that you'll have unfrozen drinking water at night and first thing in the morning. Sleep with it/them in your bag for a toasty treat or if the tent's interior will get really cold. If the tent's interior will stay near freezing, leave the bottle next to your sleeping bag or between you and your partner. Either way, your water bottle must be completely trustworthy. If you leave it loose in the tent where it might freeze, make sure it's not full or it might burst.

Bring your boots inside the sleeping bag only if it's really cold, if your feet get cold easily, or if your leather boots have enough moisture in them to freeze or stay chilled. If you're wearing plastic boots, just bring the liners inside your bag. But beware that it can sometimes be nearly impossible to get liners back into a pair of frozen plastic boots. Under moderate winter conditions, you should be okay if you've simply brought your boots into the tent for the night.

Settling in for a Winter's Night

If your busy home life leaves you a little sleep-deprived, consider taking up winter camping just for the opportunity to catch a few ZZZs. Unless your habit is to build a fire and revel with your friends until the wee hours, you'll have plenty of horizontal time during long winter nights. Of course, in order to sleep you have to be warm.

Tricks for a Warmer Night

Climb into your bag as soon as possible. If you're cooking in your vestibule, get into your bag immediately after stockpiling chunks of ice and otherwise attending to outdoor camp chores.

Fill a bottle or two with hot water and slip them into your bag. Besides a toe warmer, you'll also have water available for night drinking and for a quicker cup of morning joe. Inside your bag, the bottles will stay warm for a long time and add considerable heat. Just remember that you're running a big risk if you don't trust the seal 100 percent.

Make sure that you only enter your bag wearing dry clothes. To warm up quickly, change into dry long underwear, if you've packed an extra set, and snuggle into your bag. If your underwear is a bit damp, hang out in the tent for a while to let your body heat dry it before you get into the bag. If it's really wet (unlikely with synthetics) and you don't have a change, strip before entering your bag and hang the garments on a line to dry as best they can. To save yourself a shock when you put them back on in the morning, bring them into your bag in the morning for a while to heat up (preferably inside a plastic bag or stuff sack so they don't get the bag wet).

Wear your long underwear at night. This adds a small amount of insulation, but mostly it keeps a nice layer of warm air wrapped snugly around your body and eliminates any drafts that might otherwise disturb your slumber. How much help you can get from wearing even more layers of clothing is debated. Generally, the rule is not to overdress because you won't benefit as much from reflected or re-radiated heat from the bag. But if your bag just isn't cutting the muster, put on everything you've got that's dry—it's worth a try.

Dry socks and a hat are probably the most important things you can wear to bed to give yourself a few extra degrees of comfort, especially if the sleeping bag hood doesn't fit you perfectly or if you can't stand having it drawn snugly around your face. A balaclava does an even better job.

Take the time to adjust and snug-tight your draft collar and your hood. Do it early—better to loosen the hood because you're a little too warm than to wake up cold and have to compensate for the chill.

If you do wake up chilled, do what it takes to overcome the cold. Don't try to tough it out—the night keeps getting colder until just after

Try to bring as much gear as possible inside, and position what has to remain outside so that you can find it even after a blizzard. Plant skis firmly into the snow and attach other items to the skis. (Photo: ©John Harlin)

dawn. Of course, sometimes it takes a little while for your body's thermostat to adjust, and this is something you'll have to learn about yourself.

Drink something warm before going to sleep. But don't drink too much, because peeing in the night is a nuisance. Have some snacks on hand. This is actually one of the most important rules, because frequent munching helps enormously with your metabolism's ability to generate heat through the night. If you wake up cool, eat part or all of a candy bar or other quick-energy snack. Be sure to bring some "midnight snacks" into the tent just for this purpose. The bears you might worry about attracting in the summer will likely be hibernating at this time of year.

Don't drink alcohol. Alcohol stimulates your body to put more blood at its perimeters, where it cools faster, at the expense of your core. You might temporarily feel warmer when in fact you're chilling more quickly and more deeply.

Don't breathe into your bag, at least not for long. When I was young and camped with a too-thin bag, I always kept my head inside and I swore that my breath heated the bag. While this trick might work to help you get through a cool night in an inadequate bag, it puts too much moisture inside while winter camping. That moisture builds up in the insulation and over the course of one or more nights decreases the bag's efficiency. Still, I occasionally do this if I'm really chilled when I first crawl inside.

Think twice about zipping two bags together. If you and your loved one want to cozy up at night, consider buying or making a V-shaped insert half the size of a sleeping bag. Zip this insert to a regular bag and you have a one-and-a-half-size bag, perfect for two people. Two bags zipped together leave too much empty space that must be heated—you'll actually be colder together than apart. Also, together you can't cinch the hoods and draft collars, which makes even the insert-approach inefficient. You may feel there's more to love than heat efficiency—until, that is, the frost starts forming inside your tent.

Consider using a pee bottle, as discussed in the Sanitation section above. The fewer times you have to get dressed, unzip the tent, go outside, and then return and track snow inside, the better—never mind waking your partner each time. So drink enough to stay hydrated, because hydration is vital for staving off frostbite. But don't carry this rule to excess, at least not in the evening. Drink hearty come the morning.

BREAKING CAMP

With the sun streaming into your tent door and baking the walls, and your clothing and boots warm because you've brought them into the sleeping bag first thing in the morning (or slept with them all night), getting up on a frosty morning can be a joyful experience. In a howling snowstorm, however, or in a darkly forested deep-freeze pocket, your tent's sanctuary might be nigh-on impossible to exit, let alone dismantle. Keep in mind that once you're packed and on the move, you'll warm up quickly and inertia will be in your favor instead of working against you.

When you're lying in your bag by the dawn's early light, however, inertia is definitely your enemy. If you're not in a hurry to get somewhere, don't rush the morning process. You'll feel much better about heading out once you've been lying around long enough for boredom to set in. Even if you can't wait that long, at least wait for your mind and body to be ready to take on the challenge. Put all your clothes on when you go out into the cold, but try to have a thick insulating layer—like a down jacket—on so that it's easily removable once you're ready to throw your pack on your back and head up the trail.

You'll need some kind of liner gloves for manipulating cold tent poles, stuffing the pack, et cetera. Remember that early morning can be the coldest time of the day; be sure not to freeze your fingers during the intensely manual packing-up process.

Breakfast

Because you'll need to be well hydrated to help with blood circulation and to prevent frostbite, and because drinking cold beverages won't be tops on your list out there in the cold, be sure to drink as much water in the morning as you possibly can. Drink water from your overnight bottle before leaving the tent and beginning to cook breakfast. Then drink hot beverages during and after breakfast.

Taking Down the Tent

A minor caution is not to leave your tent sitting in its overnight spot for long while you brew up breakfast outside—the body heat–softened snow might refreeze, gluing your tent fast to the ground. With a freestanding tent, tip it sideways for a while, ideally facing the bottom into the sun.

Pulling Apart Camp

There's little that's special to breaking a winter camp that wasn't covered in chapter 1. But don't assume that a snowfall will soon obliterate signs of your camp. Remember the primary rule of the sensitive camper: Leave as little trace of your passage as possible. Fill in holes and dismantle snow walls. Pretty simple stuff.

Index

Other titles you may enjoy from The Mountaineers:

EVERYDAY WISDOM: 1001 Expert Tips for Hikers, *Karen Berger*
Expert tips and tricks for hikers and backpackers covering everything from
packing and planning to field repairs and emergency improvisations.

GORP, GLOP, AND GLUE STEW: Favorite Foods From 165 Outdoor
Experts, *Yvonne Prater & Ruth Dyar Mendenhall*
Well-known outdoor folk share favorite recipes.

STAYING FOUND, 2nd Ed.: The Complete Map and Compass Handbook,
June Fleming
Presents an easy-to-use, unified map-and-compass system. Includes instruc-
tion on route planning, and winter navigation.

▲ ▲ ▲

The mission of *BACKPACKER* magazine is to distribute, in a variety of
media, credible, in-depth, and compelling "how-to-do-it" information about
wilderness recreation, primarily in North America.

BACKPACKER
THE MAGAZINE OF WILDERNESS TRAVEL

BACKPACKER magazine
33 East Minor Street
Emmaus, PA 18098
phone: 1-610-967-5171 / fax: 1-610-967-8181
web address: www.hpbasecamp.com

THE MOUNTAINEERS, founded in 1906, is a Seattle-based non-
profit outdoor activity and conservation club with 15,000 members, whose
mission is "to explore, study, preserve, and enjoy the natural beauty of the
outdoors . . . ." The club sponsors many classes and year-round outdoor activities in the Pacific Northwest, and supports environmental causes by spon-
soring legislation and presenting educational programs. The Mountaineers
Books supports the club's mission by publishing travel and natural history
guides, instructional texts, and works on conservation and history.

Send or call for our catalog of more than 300 outdoor titles:

The Mountaineers Books
1001 SW Klickitat Way, Suite 201
Seattle, WA 98134
1-800-553-4453 / e-mail: mbooks@mountaineers.org